# FAIL
## BRILLIANTLY

FAMILIUS

Published by Familius LLC, www.familius.com

Familius books are available at special discounts for bulk purchases, whether for sales promotions or for family or corporate use. For more information, contact Familius Sales at 559-876-2170 or email orders@familius.com.

Library of Congress Cataloging-in-Publication Data
2017941394

Print ISBN 9781945547256
Ebook ISBN 9781945547614

Printed in the United States of America

Edited by Katharine Hale
Cover design by David Miles
Book design by Brooke Jorden

10 9 8 7 6 5 4 3 2 1

First Edition

# FAIL
# BRILLIANTLY

## EXPLODING THE
## MYTHS OF FAILURE
## AND SUCCESS

SHELLEY DAVIDOW, DCA
AND PAUL WILLIAMS, PHD

If you've ever felt like a failure,
this book is for you.

# CONTENTS

"I have not failed. I've just found 10,000 ways that won't work."

—Thomas Edison

"*Failure* is just another name for much of real life."

—Margaret Atwood

"There are scads of self-help books on how to succeed, but I've never come across a single one on how to contend with not succeeding—which is more the form for practically everybody, right?"

—Lionel Shriver

# FROM BLUNDERS TO CATASTROPHES:

## THE UNEXPECTED OUTCOME AS A FORCE THAT SHAPES US

**D**espite your best efforts and learning from past failures, you have failed to become the success you dreamt of being. You have pasted "Never Give Up" signs on your bathroom mirror, and you feel you have been at it 24/7 since you were at school. But after bad luck and a series of unanticipated disasters in this competitive world, you realise that there is the very real possibility that "this is it." The successful life you have imagined for yourself may never materialise.

So now what?

We live in a binary world of success and failure. Many of us wouldn't just think of ourselves as "on the road"—living through and facing adversity and making the best of what comes to us.

We most often think of ourselves as either successes or as failures. But we're caught in an illusion. We're not on a journey to a single successful destination. We're just on a journey, though we're taught every day by society to measure our lives against our expectations and the expectations of others. And much of this causes us pain—from the time we set foot in a school classroom, to the time we don't get the job we interviewed for, to the time we lose all our money on a tumbling stock market. We spend time beating ourselves up about poor decisions, about not succeeding, and we transfer that to our colleagues, our partners, our children.

Our mammal brains drive us towards the taste of success. Our so-called "failures" can paralyse us because we are wired to avoid things that cause disappointment. Though bloggers and psychologists rave on about the gifts of failure, it is still essentially a societal negative. The world frowns on us getting things wrong. We are constantly graded and branded according to the evidence of our successes: academic achievement, social standing, the cars we drive, how much money we make.

Yet the fabric of failure is an intricate and essential aspect of our existence.

Big failures often result in side events that aren't measurable: transformation, shifts in perspective and values—even if the goals themselves are never reached. From doomed explorers to aborted moon landings to novels that were rejected a dozen times, this book looks at failure as an integral part of human existence and dissolves many of the illusions surrounding failure that we have come to believe. It reveals a new approach to contending with all kinds of failures.

# DEGREES OF FAILURE

One significant problem we face is that we use *failure* as a blanket term, which can be very confusing because not all failures are created equal. When we talk about failure these days, we lump everything together as if a failed test or business venture has the same value or impact as a failed medical intervention or the failure of an aircraft to arrive at its destination.

So for the purpose of clarity, we have divided failure into three broad categories, which allows us to look at these so-called failures in new ways.

## FIRST-DEGREE FAILURES . . .

are the most devastating. These are the failures that result in total disasters and loss of life—for example: planes that fail to make it to their destinations; medical errors that result in someone dying or being irrevocably harmed; failure of an emergency service to arrive on time, resulting in disaster; failure of justice, resulting in the wrong person being convicted of a crime.

These failures have irredeemable results. People die; things are damaged beyond repair. We can hardly celebrate these failures or commend the people involved as having failed brilliantly. If we learn anything from them, it is that, at all costs, we want to prevent similar failures from happening ever again.

## SECOND-DEGREE FAILURES . . .

are those where a significant goal is set but not met. For example, the Apollo 13 mission to the moon, which was aborted but did not result in any loss of life, or Ernest Shackleton's 1914–1916 doomed voyage across Antarctica—all twenty-eight men on the journey lived, though they lost everything and never achieved their goal of crossing the continent. These second-degree failures are the adventurous or scientific journeys where one outcome is expected but another unforeseen one occurs; they are the failures of artists and researchers and writers and anyone trying to create something that has not been created before.

These failures, unlike first-degree failures, often spawn unexpected innovations, collaborations, and new ideas and lead to personal growth, development, hidden benefits, and lessons of a kind that only surviving the harshest circumstances can. These failures are commendable as having intrinsic value, as being catalysts for transformation, as bringing new and valuable knowledge to the world. They are worth celebrating. In fact, these failures should not even be termed "failures," because they bypass all the word's carefully constructed definitions.

## THIRD-DEGREE FAILURES . . .

are the ones *we* decide are failures. They are distinctly subjective, and our responses to them have as much to do with biology and physiology as with the actual failure itself. They are the failed tests, the failure to get into the university course of our choice, the failure to make enough money, or create a successful business, or be a successful writer, or meet specific targets set by our bosses or ourselves. These failures often make us feel terrible about ourselves. We are frequently unable to separate ourselves and our own value from these failures.

These failures have parameters that are randomly imposed by us, and the line dividing a so-called pass or success from failure is drawn whimsically wherever we think to draw it. When we set ourselves goals—personal, financial, academic—we unconsciously create a system of potential failures, and so it's best to understand the risk inherent in aiming for success.

Malcolm Gladwell thoroughly points out in his book *Outliers* that the people, the athletes, the social entrepreneurs,

the businessmen who succeed in terms of our material definitions of success in the world do work hard—but in every case he
examines, there exists a lucky break, a chance meeting that led
to that hard work paying off. And he demonstrates how there
are those geniuses who never got the lucky break, still living
their unremarkable lives despite their brilliance and hard work.
Their incredible ideas and creations never saw the light of day
or resulted in material success. It's a fact: bad luck and twists of
fate have prevented many talented human beings from being
rewarded for their efforts, either financially or in terms of recognition.[2] Most of us can probably identify with that to some
degree.

There is an element of chance in every so-called "success,"
and those of us who believe that we can achieve anything if we
set our minds to it need to understand that life is full of surprises
that may make our journey's outcome entirely unexpected. So
what do those of us do who have put in our ten thousand hours
towards achieving our goal and are not adequately rewarded for
our efforts?

Dealing with these "failures" requires a complete rethink of
the concept of failure—and, of course, the concept of success.

*Life is failure.* Our entire four-billion-year journey through
the universe is made up of all kinds of trials and errors. Our lives
are full of stumbles and falls and unexpected outcomes which
often do not lead to success of any kind.

We believe failure falls broadly into three categories. In this
book, we explore how these play out in the world, examine the
impact of failure on our own lives, and show how we can separate ourselves from a concept that causes unnecessary pain by
providing readers with revolutionary ways of thinking about
failure.

## NOTES

1. Yactayo-Changa, Jessica P., Sangwoong Yoon, Keat Thomas Teoh, Nathan C. Hood, Argelia Lorence, and Elizabeth E. Hood. "Failure to over-express expansion in multiple heterologous systems." *New Negatives in Plant Science* 3–4, August–December (2016): 10–18. Accessed March 16, 2017. http://www.sciencedirect.com/science/article/pii/S2352026416300022.
2. Gladwell, Malcolm. *Outliers: The Story of Success.* New York: Little, Brown and Company, 2006.

# CHAPTER ONE

# OUR PREHISTORIC ANCESTORS AND THE NEUROBIOLOGY OF FAILURE

**W**hen we think of success and failure, we are usually confined to a very specific arena: that of human endeavour to get to the top of the pile or, more plainly, to survive. Anything linked to our survival results in us experiencing the feel-good effects of serotonin, dopamine, endorphins, and oxytocin. Anything that poses a threat to our survival gets us feeling stressed, depressed, and unhappy and results eventually in low self-esteem. We want to survive. We want to thrive. In fact, we are the offspring of generations of people who were savvy enough to survive.[1]

Imagine a prehistoric ancestor wandering through the African savanna. For days, he hasn't eaten. He's been hunting a wounded antelope that he shot with his arrow, following its footprints. He's tired, he's starving, he's thirsty, and he is at least a whole day's walk from home. His children and their mother are hungry, and he really cannot do this much longer. But he persists. Suddenly, he comes upon the animal in a clearing. He is euphoric. Now he knows he and his family will have plenty to eat for the next few days. His hard work of tracking and persevering has paid off. He feels important, successful, relieved.

Our circumstances have changed and our brains have evolved over thousands of years, but essential characteristics remain almost identical to those of our prehistoric ancestors. In the modern world, that ancestor's offspring is a real estate agent. For months, she hasn't sold anything. A potential buyer for a million-dollar home in the area has been interested but not committed. For weeks, she has been showing and reshowing the house, getting information to the buyers, keeping calm when they made unreasonable requests, calling them up when their interest seemed to have waned. And then, finally, they arrive one day with their cash offer. They close the deal on the house, and she can hardly believe it. Just like her prehistoric ancestor who found food after days of hunger, she is euphoric. Her family will eat. She can get her car fixed. She can go on holiday and even visit her ailing parents overseas. She feels completely successful. She will survive!

Our brains are finely tuned for success, only now we equate good grades, money, and having lots of stuff with survival. To some degree, that is true: we're no longer wandering the plains hunting for food and sleeping in caves. We need a certain amount of money to put a roof over our heads and food on the table, but we raise the bar higher and higher, feeling deserving of more and more and better and better. We set ourselves up for feeling like failures when we don't keep climbing the ladder of material success, of having bigger houses, new cars, and more and more stuff. And then, from the minute our kids begin to breathe, we put pressure on them to achieve, to constantly move up the ladder we've created as we tick off the list of academic achievements. Without even knowing it, we tie those achievements to survival: getting an A on a spelling test in primary school begins to carry the weight of survival. It becomes a life-or-death stress for us and for our children. We believe somehow that this will be a predictor of whether they survive or not in the world.

## THE EFFECTS OF FAILURE ON ANIMALS

According to neurobiologist and author Loretta Graziano Breuning, the majority of animals suffer less from disappointment than humans do because they don't live with the expectations that things should be different.[2] Let's say you're a mongoose and a predator eats your baby. You will of course be heartbroken, you may be sad and stressed and afraid of those predators, but you won't develop elaborate theories of *self-doubt or hatred* because you failed to protect your young. As humans, our self-doubt and theories of failure in the world are added stressors that make life miserable for many.

We have a unique capacity to imagine others' suffering and to live into it. Mirror neurons allow us to feel the pain of other living creatures experiencing pain. Because of empathy with fellow humans and other living things, many of us like to imagine a more peaceful world. We can picture a world where we don't drop bombs on each other or each other's children . . . we have seen the good traits in so many people that we have the basis for hoping or even expecting that people will behave in a civilised, ethical manner—not grab each other's stuff, countries, oil, or gold. When that doesn't happen, when our expectations of how things should be are thwarted, we are devastated. When we expect our kids to pass their driving test and they don't, we might feel we've failed as parents or our children have failed. There are plenty of parents who treat kids' soccer as a life-or-death game where winning is tied closely to the self-esteem of both kids and their parents. And if their kids lose, those parents make them feel like failures. In fact, the moms and dads themselves go on to feel like failures.

But this is a system we have invented.

Those parents have tied their ancient survival instincts to a child playing a soccer game, therefore failing to win results in enormous distress that is not equal to its reality.

Other mammals have many problems—they suffer, they may be stressed—but they do not have an elaborate process for creating self-doubt. Breuning expands on this in her book *Habits of a Happy Brain* with a quote that might serve us well in many circumstances in life:

> When a monkey loses a banana to a rival, he feels bad, but he doesn't expand the problem by thinking about it over and over. He looks for another banana. He ends up feeling rewarded rather than harmed. Humans use their extra neurons to construct theories about bananas and end up constructing pain.[3]

Losing one banana is no big deal. But research suggests that over time, the loser effect kicks in. When this becomes chronic, stress levels rise. If the monkey constantly loses his banana to a more powerful monkey, if he is harassed and hounded for his banana repetitively, this has far-reaching physiological effects.

A monkey who manages to steal a ripe banana from his rival is the winner, and the loser is crushed. The winner experiences a surge in testosterone, while the loser has a significant drop. The winner, then, feels a boost of confidence and bravado, making him more likely to feel like he wants to go on and win more. In fact, if he takes on an opponent stronger than himself in a fight, he will likely win, because his success has primed him to do so. The loser who scuttles off beaten is more likely to be a loser again the next time around.[4]

Human primates experience the same rush of testosterone and endorphins or dopamine when we succeed at small tasks as nonhuman primates do, and how this plays out in our own lives is interesting. We are, after all, not that different physiologically from our primate friends. Neuroscientist Robert Sapolsky shows in his book *Why Zebras Don't Get Ulcers* that our socio-economic status has direct correlations to our health, and that in the primate world, the high-ranking baboons, for example, have a far healthier stress response and suffer less from all kinds of health issues than lower-ranking baboons.[5] This has to do with how much the subordinate baboon is harassed, picked on, and attacked. Baboons and other primates who are aggravated by others and made to feel inferior have higher cortisol levels and higher glucocorticoid levels, and they consequently live shorter lives. The difference between nonhuman primates and us is almost nonexistent in one sense: we live longer the more successful we *feel*. *Feeling* poor and subordinate is a predictor of a shorter life span.[6] But there is an enormous difference between us in another sense: as thinking human beings with the capacity to imagine, project, and compare, we *do* have control over our responses to the world.

This is probably one of the most intriguing revelations because it means that the external reality has a measurable effect that affects our health. Being able to generate a positive outlook when the world is falling on our heads is next to impossible—but if we know that our responses to our circumstances play a significant part in our overall health, we can do our best to be kind to ourselves, to take steps to minimise stress as much as possible, to understand that sometimes our only freedom is how we react to the things that life throws at us.

## CHANGING THE WAY WE LOOK AT FAILURE

This is the problem with our concept of failure: *feeling* like we've failed in our socially induced hierarchy of "What Is Important" creates physiological effects that can affect our lives negatively, even shorten them. We could apply this to all third-degree failures: *I feel terrible because I failed the math exam. I feel terrible because I failed to get the job promotion. I feel like a failure because I've been working hard every single day of my life and I still drive a ten-year-old Toyota and can't afford to get a new car.* This is not the case with most second-degree failures, since the journey is most often known to be a risky one where failure is even anticipated and where the adventure offers up lessons and valuable insights that don't leave the adventurers feeling crushed.

For example: In 2016, two young entrepreneurs from very different companies (SpaceX Chief Executive Elon Musk and Facebook's Mark Zuckerberg) decided to work together, pool resources, and launch a satellite at Cape Canaveral. They had great hopes that their venture would bring the internet to remote villages in Africa. But as they watched, the multimillion-dollar, 604-ton Falcon 9 rocket exploded on the launch pad, destroying the expensive satellite on board. They could have felt as if this event was a personal failure, but they took the position that the failure was part of a process. They hoped to find out what went wrong so that it hopefully would not happen again.[7]

Feelings of being less worthy come about because we are smart enough to invent the idea of failure. If we can create our own complex theories of failure and success based on comparison, surely we can redesign our concept.

Marge Denver,[8] a schoolteacher in Florida with twenty years of expert teaching under her belt, was well aware of this "feeling less than" and the negative implications for health. For the past eighteen months, her immediate superior had been subtly harassing and undermining her. Whereas before she'd loved her job, suddenly she dreaded each day, dreaded meetings, dreaded running into the man harassing her. Then a new head was hired in the school, and his autocratic approach dovetailed exactly with her immediate superior. Now she had two men actively bullying her at every turn. She watched her stress levels rising.

Her health suffered. She thought about suing them for harassment, but then she realised that this action would result in elevated stress for her over a prolonged period of time.

In a single moment, she decided that the cost to her own personal happiness had tipped the balance. She resigned on the spot and began the long search for a new job, feeling that the stress of being unemployed for a while was less than the stress of doing battle with her sexist superiors. She understood that feeling harassed was more detrimental than proactively searching for a more suitable job and would probably have a measurable impact on her life expectancy. She didn't feel like a failure anymore; she felt like someone with agency. She made a choice after a personal cost-benefit analysis of the situation and decided that the cost of staying was much higher than the emotional and physiological cost of leaving, and she bet on taking the route that would have the most positive outcome for her at that moment, despite its risks.

This could look like a failure: Marge resigned from her job, and she failed to make the men responsible for her misery accountable; or it could be a success: her anxiety vanished immediately. Her feelings of low self-worth were entirely circumstantial, so she now felt empowered, liberated, and ready for a new challenge and a new phase.

Our feelings of failure can cause us distress. The way we reflect on our lives and the context we create for ourselves generate our disposition and our attitude toward unexpected outcomes. When we lose things that we need or want, we have an immediate physiological, emotional, and psychological response—a gut reaction to the loss or lack of achievement. But here's where we have the power to affect our lives: our thoughts about not getting what we want, our response to the unanticipated outcome, can be changed. Our emotions and bodies will respond accordingly.

As self-conscious, self-aware beings with the capacity to

change our minds and our thoughts, we can decide whether we are going to beat ourselves up about losing the banana, the business deal, or the job or whether we are going to move on and look for another banana, business deal, or job.

In acknowledging that our enterprising nature, our quest for survival, is deeply rooted in our desire for material success, we can look at failure through a clear lens: as a species, we have not changed very much in the last forty thousand years, but our lives have transformed entirely. We desire things that make us feel safe and signal to us that we will survive. We save money in our bank accounts for a rainy day. But all too often, the more money we have, the more we think we need. For the majority of people, the goalposts shift constantly. There are numerous levels and ways of being in the world, and our physical and material needs represent only one aspect. Feeling materially secure is an individual state of being which varies significantly between individuals. There is no objective set of criteria that we can use to measure a person's so-called success or failure.

We make these measurements and criteria up: we decide that someone who drives an Audi is somehow more successful, more likely to thrive and survive, than someone who drives a ten-year-old Toyota. But that's because we have substituted a biological evolutionary function (the drive to survive) with material stuff, and somehow we have made the Audi a representative of that success.

Let's look at a hypothetical scenario that represents someone most of us would know. Imagine that the driver of that luxury car, Kian, is stressed out. In two days' time, he will suffer a massive heart attack. He is not feeling well. He has been fighting with his wife, his kids seem ungrateful, and he is feeling poor compared to Barney, an old school friend who has invented a telecommunication device and made millions over the past seven years. Kian regrets not going into business with this guy ten years ago when he was given the opportunity. He feels like he made a gross error of judgment back then and has paid for it every day since Barney's huge success. Kian's arteries are clogged. His blood pressure is high. He has lost interest in everything and can focus only on the fact that he hasn't lived up to his own expectations of himself. He feels like a failure, and this has ingrained itself into his behaviour; it has become the baseline for where his thoughts go every minute of the day. His goal when he graduated was simply to achieve enough material wealth in order to survive and live a long and happy life, but that has slowly been misplaced. If his impulse hadn't been hijacked by his moving of goalposts and his comparison of himself to others, he would not be sitting at a traffic light at forty-two years old, forty-eight hours away from a heart attack.

When we look at what's happening in our brains, in Kian's pattern of thought, we can easily see that perhaps if he had focused on other things until this point—enjoyed life, had fun, taken care of his relationships and health, and had a slightly different perspective and relationship to his material goals—things might have gone very differently. Every single day until this point, he had the power to change his perception: he already had enough to survive. But he made a constant comparison to his classmate and didn't understand that he could have altered the emotional and physiological responses he had when he didn't get what he wanted.

In basic terms, he didn't even lose his banana. He just saw that someone else had more bananas. This made him dissatisfied with everything he had. With a single thought, he could have dissolved the ladder of so-called success he had created.

Dissolving imaginary ladders and hierarchies is a uniquely human capacity. We have created an invisible reality based on an evolutionary instinct that we now believe in. We've made a story, and now we actually believe in the symbols of success and failure generated by the media and social construction. But if we stand back, we can change our experience of reality with our thoughts. If we have the capacity to create these ladders, we have the capacity to take them down. We can decide what to value and what to treasure; we can decide not to buy into a perception of some people as losers and others as winners. The repercussions of this could be far reaching.

Feeling like a loser is dangerous and the physiological outcomes of the "loser effect" can be so profound that they can shorten our lives. Feeling less worthy (or bullied or picked on) has the same effect on us as it does on our baboon buddies; our levels of glucocorticoids rise and we are likely to suffer from hypertension and other immediate stress-related ailments.

This "keeping up with the Joneses" affects people in both poor and rich countries. It seems to be that in terms of feeling happy and wealthy, actual income doesn't have as great an impact as relative income. Being surrounded by wealthier, more powerful, more enabled neighbours makes us feel like we're not keeping up, regardless of whether we're earning $3,000 per year or $3,000,000. This comparative, competitive aspect to our lives is something we can be aware of and have control of. The psychological and emotional component of feeling worthless, which belongs to both us and nonhuman primates, is a powerful force. We so often create situations for ourselves like Kian did in which we imagine ourselves to be less worthy and in which we will never find happiness, because there will always be those who are materially richer and more successful than we are.

As busy, striving human beings, constantly trying to progress in one way or another, often under pressure to perform by bosses who demand certain outcomes, plagued by financial stresses, by unexpected expenses and disasters that make us feel overwhelmed, we can find ourselves going down one of a few possible paths:

1.  We give up. We believe we've failed or we are not equal to the task. We escape into drink, drugs, destructive behaviours. We feel like losers, and we are primed for

the next bad thing to happen and knock us down even further. Our stress levels rise. Blood pressure rises. The loser effect kicks in, and our risk for living a shorter life increases.

2. We see the outcome as a motivator. Fuelled by the desire and commitment to not let this get us down, we come back at the world with vigour and determination to keep on, regardless of how long it takes.

3. We accept the absolute uncertainty of every single adventure in our lives. We understand that destinations change constantly and that life will throw us unexpected events frequently. So we learn about changing direction, changing our thoughts, shifting our perceptions of a situation, and reevaluating our lives and our present situations without judging ourselves or measuring our worth in terms of success and failure.

The point is: if we were clever enough to create the idea of failure in the first place, and if our survival depends to some degree on us not feeling as though we are failures, then we're surely smart enough to erase the common idea of failure—a concept we'll explore in detail later when we look at the language of failure, the stories we tell ourselves, our philosophies of failure, and how we can begin to rewrite our narratives and shift our point of view.

## BIG IDEAS

▶ Our ideas of success and failure are based on a primal survival instinct.

▶ Low-ranking primates in the animal kingdom have higher stress levels and often live shorter lives.

▶ Feeling like a loser can raise stress levels and affect health.

► We have invented the idea of personal failure with
often-disastrous effects.
► We are smart enough to erase the idea of so-called
personal failures and live longer, happier lives.

## NOTES

1. Breuning, Loretta Graziano. *Habits of a Happy Brain: Retrain Your Brain to Boost Your Serotonin, Dopamine, Oxytocin & Endorphin Levels.* Avon, MA: Adams Media, 2016. 12.
2. Ibid., 16.
3. Ibid., 30.
4. Robertson, Ian H. *The Winner Effect: The Neuroscience of Success and Failure.* New York: Thomas Dunne Books, 2012. 3–20.
5. Sapolsky, Robert M. *Why Zebras Don't Get Ulcers: An Updated Guide to Stress, Stress-Related Diseases, and Coping,* 2nd Edition. New York: W. H. Freeman and Co., 1998. 7.
6. Sapolsky, Robert. "Sick of Poverty." *Scientific American* 293, no. 6 (2005): 92–99.
7. Masunaga, Samantha, and Jim Puzzanghera. "SpaceX explosion frustrates both Elon Musk's and Mark Zuckerberg's plans." *Los Angeles Times*, September 1, 2016. http://www.latimes.com/business/la-fi-space-x-explosion-20160901-snap-story.html.
8. Marge Denver. Interview with authors. 2017. Name changed for privacy.

## SUGGESTED READING

DeBord, Matthew. "Elon Musk is setting himself up for an epic failure." *Business Insider Australia*, May 9, 2016. Accessed August 4, 2016. http://www.businessinsider.com.au/musk-epic-failure-2016-5?r=US&IR=T.

# CHAPTER TWO

# FIRST-DEGREE FAILURES:

## CATASTROPHES OF THE LAST ONE HUNDRED YEARS

**G**o into any bookstore and you will easily find shelves of books on how to embrace failure, fail more, fail better, learn from failure, make failure your friend, and discover value in failure—all with the idea that if you aren't failing, somehow you aren't putting in the effort, so to speak. But failure of this nature belongs in a special category. The word itself, as we are coming to see, is problematic because not all failures are equal.

First-degree failures are not the subject of these books and are not failures we want to experience more of, but they have always happened and will continue to happen. We may learn from them, but there is only one lesson: how to try to avoid this in the future. The benefits of these failures, if any are to be had, belong to succeeding generations, to those who come after.

The TV series *Air Crash Investigations*[1] is a program based on just this: what errors led to the disaster, and what will be done so that this does not happen again? The details are unimportant, and the idea is applied to all commissions of enquiry: *What went wrong? Can we avoid this particular event happening again in the future?*

Perhaps this is valuable, but in some instances, we'd have to ask: *Could this have been avoided in the first place? Are the lessons we learn worth the price some pay? In fact, can we ever say that what we gain from first-degree failures is worth the price?*

# FAMOUS FIRST-DEGREE FAILURES

Let's look at some first-degree failures from the last one hundred years. These are catastrophes. First-degree failures of the twentieth century include preventable accidents, many of which involve the destruction of ships, aircraft, and buildings with significant loss of human life.

The so-called unsinkable *Titanic* hit an iceberg and went down in 1912. It turned out that the brittle fracture of both rivets and the hull steel due to freezing temperatures, high sulphur content, and high impact led to the giant ship buckling and then breaking up. The design flaw of the watertight compartments being watertight only horizontally led to them filling rapidly with water, pitching, and then sinking the ship faster than if there had been no compartments at all, which would have enabled the water to spread out, left the ship horizontal, and possibly given passengers more time to escape. Many passengers drowned who shouldn't have, had safety measures been adequate—especially when it came to lifeboats. Although the *Titanic* had enough lifeboats to fulfil the regulations at the time, there were only enough for just over half the passengers. An entire row of lifeboats had been removed prior to the ship sailing to make the deck area more spacious. To make matters worse, the lifeboats that were available took time to launch and were not filled to capacity.[2] Boats with the capacity for forty people were launched with only twelve on board. As a result of these oversights, only 32 percent of the passengers survived.

Many changes were made post-*Titanic* that lessened the negative outcomes of future disasters: sister ships had redesigned hulls where the watertight compartments, if punctured, would allow for water to fill horizontally and spread out, keeping the ship level rather than flowing over the tops of the bulkheads; cruisers were outfitted with enough lifeboats to carry *all* passengers; and rocket signals from ships were to be interpreted *only* as distress signals and calls for help. (Apparently, a passing freighter, the SS *Californian*, had observed rockets being fired from the distant, sinking *Titanic* but had interpreted the flares as identification or "company signals," used to show other freighters where they were!) Ice patrol ships and then planes were used to keep an eye on vast areas of ocean, and, of course, there were several amendments to hull design in general, including the now well-known double hull.[3]

Another tragedy during the first half of the twentieth century happened when the *Hindenberg* airship blew up in front of passenger family members, friends, and the public in May 1937. For three decades, airship travel had been a luxurious and exciting pastime, but the *Hindenberg* disaster brought this all to an end. After flying into a thunderstorm with one hundred passengers and crew on board, a buildup of static electricity and a broken wire or valve led to hydrogen leaking into ventilation shafts as the airship came to land in New Jersey. The hydrogen immediately ignited, resulting in a fire that killed thirty-five passengers and crew as well as a man on the ground. The fact that the tragedy was caught on film and broadcast around the world captured people's imagination. They viewed it with horror. No one wanted to travel on an airship again, and this disaster marked the end of the airship age. Though there are a few dirigibles still flying, such as the Goodyear Blimp and UK-designed airship/ plane/helicopter The Airlander, the gas used to lift them is not hydrogen but helium, which is not flammable.[4]

Fast-forward to the 1980s: seventy-three seconds after launching from Cape Canaveral, Florida, on a chilly morning in January 1986, the space shuttle *Challenger* exploded. Several engineers who had worked on the shuttle, as well as a few individuals at NASA, were concerned beforehand that the cold temperatures on the ground might affect the seals (O-rings) surrounding the solid rocket boosters, making them brittle and unable to prevent dangerous gas from leaking through. But "go fever" seemed to affect a few senior officials at NASA, who ignored the engineers' warnings that they had absolutely no data to show that the shuttle could take off safely. On the day of the launch, one O-ring was brittle because of the cold, while the other bent, which meant a gap formed. This allowed a clear pathway for dangerously hot (5000 degrees Fahrenheit) gas to flow through. The gap did seal itself at a certain point, but the wear and tear on the O-rings combined with unexpected wind shear resulted in an explosion of the liquid hydrogen and oxygen tank. Investigators believe that the entire crew was alive after the explosion and that they lived for the two minutes it took for the crew cabin to travel further into space in an uncontrolled trajectory before falling into the ocean. The cabin was tougher than any other component and remained intact, but it hit the ocean at such a speed and with such force that no person or thing could have survived the impact. The deaths of the seven astronauts on board, including civilian schoolteacher Christa McAuliffe, who had been planning to teach lessons from space, was a tragedy with worldwide impact. Some of the engineers on the ground who had wanted to delay liftoff said the moment the explosion occurred, they "knew exactly what had happened."[5]

The lessons learned were hard won. The errors were structural in nature, and discovering this resulted in structural changes to other shuttles—adding another O-ring, not over-loading the shuttle, and not using the shuttle for launching satellites—but they were also cultural: several people, astronauts included, had had concerns that they had been reticent to make known to the launch control team. Therefore, one of the changes implemented was that all concerns from engineers and astronauts would be heard and heeded by the launch control team.[6] At any rate, this event proved to be a costly failure at every level—one that no one wanted to see repeated, which led to sweeping changes in several areas of the space industry.

The year 1986 continued to be one of disastrous international failure. The worst nuclear accident in the world happened in Chernobyl, Ukraine, in April of that year. As workers at a power plant tested the turbines in the number four reactor, they had to power down and then power up the reactor, but it had to be done very slowly. A sudden power surge and the failure of the emergency shutdown system that followed resulted in a massive explosion. Temperatures reached 3632 degrees Fahrenheit. The 1000-ton roof of the building blew off, and the fire burned for nine days, pouring more radiation into the world than anything ever before.

Since then, tens of thousands of people have died. Those who were involved in the accident, in the cleanup afterwards (called "liquidators" because they gave up their lives to try to contain the disaster), those living in a certain radius of the plant, the children of affected parents—a countless number of people died who were directly or indirectly affected by fallout from the accident.

Anyone who has seen any footage of the surrounding area will know that humanity has the capacity to completely destroy its environment by its own failures. Officials estimate that it will take some twenty thousand years for the area to be safe to live in again—if our species hasn't "liquidated" itself in other ways by then!

Meanwhile, most of the nuclear fuel at Chernobyl still lies in the sarcophagus built to contain the number four reactor, with massive amounts of waste held in a fragile container. Some scientists fear that another nuclear disaster could happen at Chernobyl at any time.[7]

As a result of this nuclear accident, the construction of nuclear power plants worldwide decreased astronomically. Since the Chernobyl accident, only 194 reactors have been connected worldwide, as opposed to 409 reactors in the 32 years prior to the accident. After the 2011 Fukushima meltdown and leak in Japan, Germany decided to phase out all nuclear power plants by 2022, and other European countries have made significant reductions in the number of nuclear power plants in operation.[8] It is possible to imagine that if another disaster happens any time in the next few decades, people might decide that the benefits of having nuclear power may not outweigh the risks.

The effects of the disasters at Chernobyl and Fukushima demonstrate that a failure to imagine the consequences of using nuclear power could mean the end of our human race. The word *failure*, then, as a concept of terminal destruction, would be appropriate in that our species would fail to survive.

Moving into the twenty-first century, our first-degree failures seem to show no hint of slowing. But perhaps disastrous events come to light so much more frequently now because of the amount of reporting by mainstream and social media. The September 11, 2001 attacks on the Twin Towers and the Pentagon have been referred to by the 9/11 commission as a result of a colossal "failure of the imagination."[9]

No one imagined that suicide pilots could hijack passenger jets and turn them into missiles. But there had been many suicide bombings before, and intelligence had previously revealed that US foreign policy in the Middle East was causing outrage amongst many and that prior to 9/11, attacks on US nationals and icons were imminent. A previous truck bomb outside the World Trade Center in New York City and an attack on US Embassies in Kenya demonstrated that there were clearly enough individuals willing to go on suicide missions. And then there were suspected terrorists with ties to Osama bin Laden learning to fly in small airports around the country, with federal authorities aware for years that they were receiving flight training.[10]

On that fateful day, airport security failed thoroughly. Nineteen hijackers, some carrying knives, made it past people and machines onto their designated planes. What have we learned from this failure?

Security at airports and in aircraft has increased and improved exponentially. But, of course, if the failure was one of imagination, then as a society, we are perhaps not imaginative enough. If suicidal hijackers use knives on one flight and another intercepted hijacker has a bomb in his shoe on a later flight, then it is probable that even if everyone takes off their shoes and has a full-body scan, the next attack will be something unanticipated.

We would be forgiven for thinking, then, that we have failed to make the world a safer place over the past fifty decades, but, in fact, this is a media-induced illusion. In *The Better Angels of Our Nature*, author Steven Pinker reveals how modernisation and our widening circles of empathy have led to the reality that despite everything we see on the news, we are much less likely to be killed by another human being than we were decades or centuries ago.[11]

# LEARNING FROM FIRST-DEGREE FAILURES

There can, of course, be a pragmatic approach to finding value in and using the lessons from first-degree failures with positive results for future generations. This approach is epitomised in the airline industry, where today's safety is built on the back of yesterday's disasters. Classic pilot errors and structural issues with aircraft that have led to fatal and near-fatal accidents have been picked apart for years. Subsequently, changes have been made either in protocol, pilot training, or tackling structural or maintenance faults that have all resulted in much safer air travel. This approach is highlighted in the program *Air Crash Investigations* and is the main theme of the book *Black Box Thinking*. Author Matthew Syed maintains that if the medical establishment treated their first-degree failures in the same way we treat air disasters, the entire profession would change.[12] He cites statistics that would make anyone think twice about going into the hospital for even a minor medical procedure: the number of people dying as a result of medical errors and failures amount to the equivalent of two jumbo jets falling out of the sky every day. And we get nervous about being blown up by terrorists on airplanes!

So whenever someone talks about failure, we must include the airline industry as a kind of blueprint for how to turn first-degree disasters into learning experiences that benefit those who come after. Case in point: Malcolm Gladwell, bestselling author of *Outliers*, explores an "ethnic theory of plane crashes" based on the fact that in the 1990s, Korean Air had more crashes than any other airline. This was due not to faulty planes or even faulty pilots but to the intensively hierarchical cultural protocols in which subordinates—in this case, copilots—would not question their superior's decisions. A combination of that and limited language capacity in English resulted in a series of fatal crashes. But as Gladwell states, once the airline realised that its problem was a cultural one, it amended its pilot training.[13] That amendment has slowly filtered into general training in aviation, and now, copilots are encouraged to take initiative and be proactive if they believe the captain to be in error.

Lessons learned from failures in aviation are examples of evolution: how we can use first-degree failures and disasters to prevent future catastrophes.

A Florida physician recently told us that she said she was acutely aware of the attitude towards failure in her profession, which is to throw a blanket of silence over the numerous medical failures that occur.[14] Unlike the airline industry, and as highlighted in *Black Box Thinking*, she said it was extraordinarily difficult for doctors to discuss failures, even at the simplest and most non–life threatening level. Perhaps this reticence is bound up with the fact that for a medical professional to acknowledge a serious error, a first-degree failure, the personal liability and responsibility would be enormous. Doctors who fail at operations live on, while most often pilots who crash passenger planes don't. Fatal air crashes result in investigations, which usually lead to an understanding of what went wrong, and if the cause was pilot error, as it often is, the pilot is no longer there to answer questions about his or her actions. This is not the case in the medical world. When we go in for a procedure, we are often asked to sign ourselves over, to promise not to hold doctors and hospitals responsible or accountable. As a result, there is little open discussion about how to avoid or prevent catastrophic medical failures, though they occur anyway.

Ultimately, the problem with catastrophic first-degree failures is that even if we make our futures safer and learn lessons from past mistakes, we can't bring back the people we've lost.

First-degree failures are terminal.

In the majority of cases, these are the only failures that are not contextual or open to interpretation.

As vulnerable human beings, we will continue to be affected by catastrophic first-degree failures into the future, despite all the safeguards in the world. This is a place where terminal occurrences are inevitable. Human-induced disasters will plague us as long as we exist on the planet. We will learn and change things, and the dangers of today may not pose much risk in the future. But new dangers will continue to arise, and we will take risks with new ventures. Some of those will end in catastrophe. We will lose people and communities as a result of human error, and this will affect millions of us.

With that in mind, it seems essential to look at first-degree failures through the eyes of a realist: given that these catastrophes will forever be part of our human world, what are we to do?

It would be naïve to assume that with enough expertise and care in various areas, we can totally eliminate tragedy and terminal outcomes. We can't. We are all mortal, for one thing, and so the idea that we can progress in medicine, aviation, science, technology, and every pathway of human endeavour without loss is an illusion.

What we need, though, are approaches to these catastrophes that enable the rest of the human race, those who are touched by these happenings, to manage themselves and their lives afterwards. In Chapter Ten, we will discuss what it means to live with the results of first-degree failures and what to do when those catastrophes affect our lives.

In light of first-degree failures, every other thing that we term a "failure" can be renamed, redesigned, and reimagined. In a world propelled by trial and error, by things that happen every day that are unexpected and unanticipated, we might do well to free ourselves from the concept of failure and replace it with something that more closely matches our lived experience and does not carry the weight of so much negative baggage.

## BIG IDEAS

- ▶ Major catastrophes have always been and will continue to be part of human evolution.
- ▶ First-degree failures are terminal—the lessons learned often do serve to make the world safer for others; this is their value. But the disaster cannot be undone.
- ▶ We are overall safer now than we were a hundred years ago, despite media messages telling us the opposite.
- ▶ We can't prevent catastrophes, but we can learn to live

in their aftermath.

► All other so-called failures are not failures—they belong to the realm of unexpected outcomes.

## HELPFUL THOUGHTS FOR LIFE AFTER FIRST-DEGREE FAILURES

► There is nothing to protect any of us from being affected by disaster.

► We can attempt to salvage lessons and insights and effect change when disaster strikes.

► We can look at our lives after disasters and know that this is what it means to be human. We have to move forward one step at a time.

► After first-degree failures, professional counselling can help us navigate this territory.

## NOTES

1. *Air Crash Investigations.* National Geographic, September, 3, 2003. Television series. Accessed March 11, 2017. http://www.national-geographic.com.au/tv/air-crash-investigation/.
2. Bassett, Vicki. "Causes and Effects of the Rapid Sinking of the Titanic." Undergraduate Engineering Review, December 2, 1998. Accessed February 22nd, 2017. http://writing.engr.psu.edu/uer/bassett.html.
3. Ibid.
4. Lawless, Jill. "Giant helium-filled airship Airlander takes off for first time." Phys.org, August 17, 2016. Accessed February 22, 2017. https://phys.org/news/2016-08-giant-helium-filled-airship-airlander.html.
5. Howell, Elizabeth. "Challenger: Shuttle Disaster That Changed NASA." Space.com, October 16, 2012. Accessed August 8, 2016. http://www.space.com/18084-space-shuttle-challenger.html.
6. Ibid.

7. "What happened in Chernobyl?" Greenpeace International, March 20, 2006. Accessed August 15, 2016. http://www.greenpeace. org/international/en/campaigns/nuclear/nomorechernobyls/ what-happened-in-chernobyl/.

8. Beale, Charlotte. "Has the Chernobyl disaster affected the number of nuclear plants built?" *The Guardian*, April 30, 2016. Accessed August 8, 2016. https://www.theguardian.com/environment/ 2016/apr/30/ has-chernobyl-disaster-affected-number-of-nuclear-plants-built.

9. "9/11 Commission Report." National Commission on Terrorist Attacks upon the United States, July 22, 2004. Accessed August 2, 2016. http://govinfo.library.unt.edu/911/report/index.htm.

10. Fainaru, Steve, and James V. Grimaldi. "FBI Knew Terrorists Were Using Flight Schools." *Washington Post*, September 23, 2001. https://www.washingtonpost.com/ archive/politics/2001/09/23/fbi-knew-terrorists-were-using- flight-schools/377177b0-b632-429f-9a15-393c2256c2b4/?utm_ term=.98275f2b7a8f.

11. Pinker, Steven. *The Better Angels of Our Nature: Why Violence Has Declined.* New York: Viking, 2011.

12. Syed, Matthew. *Black Box Thinking: Why Most People Never Learn from Their Mistakes—But Some Do.* New York: Portfolio, 2015.

13. Gladwell, *Outliers.*

14. Personal interview with the authors, 2017. Name withheld for privacy.

# CHAPTER THREE

# SECOND-DEGREE FAILURES:

## EXPLORERS, ENTREPRENEURS, AND FEEDING THE "FAIL BETTER" FRENZY

Second-degree failures belong to all of us. This is the realm of innovators, scientists, artists, engineers, writers, and anyone who sets out on an adventure, an endeavour—whether it's to go to the moon, cross Antarctica, or write a novel.

## FAMOUS SECOND-DEGREE FAILURES OF THE TWENTIETH CENTURY

### ERNEST SHACKLETON

This well-known second-degree failure happened just over one hundred years ago. In 1914, Irishman Ernest Shackleton, an experienced Antarctic explorer, set out with a crew of twenty-eight men to cross the southern continent in a powerful sailing ship, the *Endurance*, in what became known as the Imperial Trans-Antarctic Expedition. The ship became stuck in ice in the Weddell Sea before the explorers even had the chance to set foot on the landmass they wished to cross. Over many months, the ice and ship drifted more than a thousand miles north. Eventually, the pressure from the ice crushed the ship and it sank. The twenty-eight men camped out on the ice, readying the lifeboats in the event that they would need to leave. Eventually, the ice floe they were on began to break up, and they knew that they had to make a decision.

They ended up in three lifeboats, trekking across the icy ocean to Elephant Island, a cold, unwelcoming, and uninhabited place where temperatures were often below -20 degrees Celsius (-4 degrees Fahrenheit). Shackleton knew that they would only survive if they could get help. The only ships that came close to Elephant Island were whaling ships, and these were infrequent. His small party of six then decided to leave the others. They set off in a refurbished lifeboat to sail over the open and icy seas to South Georgia Island, where a whaling station meant there would be people and potential rescue ships at hand. During that voyage, the crew survived some unimaginable events. At one point, Shackleton looked up at a dark sky and saw what he thought was a streak of white light coming through a gap in the clouds. To his disbelief, he realised he was staring at the crest of a gigantic wave, which towered over them. The fact that both boat and crew survived that wave was a miracle. The other miracle was that in the weeks that followed, the navigator who was using the sun saw it only three times, briefly, and still managed to steer the craft to the edge of South Georgia Island. It took the explorers two days to land, with high winds and rough seas casting them back from the shore.

After trekking across South Georgia Island in frozen

conditions, having to climb through icy ravines not knowing if they would fall to their deaths, and having to climb down through a freezing waterfall before they finally reached the whaling station, the real rescue mission had only begun.

With the aid of large vessels from South America, Shackleton attempted to reach Elephant Island four times. Thick ice and wild weather prevented them, until finally they made it to shore and rescued the men who had been waiting for months. One had lost his left foot due to frostbite and ensuing gangrene; two ship's surgeons were on the island and performed the amputation. Other than that loss, every single one of the twenty-eight men who had set out to cross Antarctica survived.[1]

The mission had been doomed even before it began. The men never set foot on the continent they had planned to cross.

Yet the real miracle, perhaps far more impressive than any continental crossing could have been, was the tenacity and survival of these men in the most appalling of conditions and their mission to rescue themselves and each other.

The myth that we generally accept is that this voyage was a spectacular failure. Some men set out to cross a continent and failed.

But is that really the case? From another perspective, there is another reality. This was an adventure that lasted three years and revealed extraordinary human capacities to survive in the face of impossible odds. The journey was a miracle of brilliance and endurance. If we shift the point of view by a few degrees, we can see that though these men didn't achieve their original goal, they did something else. Their survival tells a human story worthy of as much admiration as any crossing of the continent could have inspired. They did not fail. Their journey and their achievements just turned out to be far different than what they had imagined.

## APOLLO 13

Another brilliant so-called failure had the world holding its breath in 1970.

For two days, three astronauts travelled into space, watching Earth diminish in size until it looked like a moon itself while the actual moon loomed large in front of them. At more than 200,000 miles from home, they were just 137 nautical miles from the moon's surface. Soon, they would make history.

Suddenly, a massive explosion blasted through the No. 2 oxygen tank, and the words of astronaut John "Jack" Swigert came through at ground control: "Houston, we've had a problem."

It may have crossed a few superstitious minds that thirteen was an unlucky number. Apollo 13, the seventh manned mission to the moon, was suddenly in grave danger on April 13, 1970. The explosion destroyed oxygen tank No. 2 and subsequently rendered the service module incapable, which was essential for the command module to function. The blast affected the No. 1 oxygen tank detrimentally as well. Renowned astronaut James Lovell recalls:

> The pressure in the No. 1 oxygen tank continued to drift downward; passing 300 psi, now heading toward 200 psi. Months later, after the accident investigation was complete, it was determined that, when the No. 2 tank blew up, it either ruptured a line on the No. 1 tank, or caused one of the valves to leak. When the pressure reached 200 psi, it was obvious that we were going to lose all oxygen, which meant that the last fuel cell would also die.[2]

At that moment, with the mountains of the moon not even one hundred fifty miles below them, their goal so close they could almost touch it, the mission to the moon was aborted. One hugely expensive endeavour became a total failure within seconds. And yet, for James A. Lovell, Jack Swigert, and Fred W.

Haise, the focus changed in an instant. Forget about the moon landing—now every single thought was attuned to a new goal: getting safely back to Earth. Lovell described the experience in his article "Houston, We've Had a Problem":

> The knot tightened in my stomach, and all regrets about not landing on the Moon vanished. Now it was strictly a case of survival. . . .[3]
>
> I did, of course, occasionally think of the possibility that the spacecraft explosion might maroon us in an enormous orbit about the Earth—a sort of perpetual monument to the space program. But Jack Swigert, Fred Haise, and I never talked about that fate during our perilous flight. I guess we were too busy struggling for survival.[4]

The astronauts had to use the sun to align the lunar module; they had to collaborate with those on the ground to find a way to deal with the issue of getting rid of carbon dioxide so that they did not die from their own exhaust fumes. In the end, they rigged up a carbon dioxide removal system imitating a blueprint made on the ground.

> Jack and I put it together: just like building a model airplane. The contraption wasn't very handsome, but it worked. It was a great improvisation—and a fine example of cooperation between ground and space.[5]

They were freezing, dehydrated, sleep deprived, and running out of everything. They didn't know that they would survive reentry if they even made it as far as the earth's atmosphere.

When they finally splashed down in the ocean, they were completely unaware that a billion people on earth were watching and living the entire saga—and that for those people, the idea of failure had changed entirely. Failure now would have meant losing the astronauts. Their ingenuity had resulted in the best possible outcome: survival of all three.

"Survive we did, but it was close," Lovell wrote. "Our mission was a failure, but I like to think it was a successful failure."[6]

Everyone, even the astronauts themselves, believed that in terms of reaching the goal they had set, the mission was a failure.

But again, if we shift our perspective, the reality was that the mission was a spectacular story of human ingenuity and survival. The goal to land on the moon transformed into the goal to get home safely. They avoided a catastrophic first-degree failure and made it back to Earth. The mission was not a failure. It just didn't pan out as expected.

# EPIC SO-CALLED FAILURES IN SCIENCE, MEDICINE, AND TECHNOLOGY

For the cohort of people who are marketing failure as a good thing, let's define that by second-degree failure, we're not talking catastrophic life-enders here. We are talking exploration and innovation in travel, business, technology, the arts, and science. In this sense, failure seems like an inadequate concept. We are looking at human endeavour, at the adventure of engaging with the world, and that always has unpredictable outcomes. The adventurers (be it explorers, car manufacturers, or inventors) have goals in mind, but they are well aware of the fact that they cannot predict the outcomes. The question would be whether these second-degree failures should be termed failures at all. Many of their unanticipated outcomes may lead to other new and evolved things and ideas. Failure isn't really failure in the grand sense when all you're doing is experimenting. It could even seem somewhat immoral to wear a badge that says "Fail Often" when all you mean is "Keep Going For It." Take this quote from an article about Elon Musk, for example: "Failure is considered a badge of honour in Silicon Valley. If you aren't failing, you aren't trying. And if you aren't failing big time, you aren't aiming high enough."[7]

Try telling that to the kid who keeps getting Ds on his spelling tests, or to the airline that keeps crashing its airplanes into the sea. Failure, as you can probably see by now, is not a singular concept.

Let's take a closer look at Musk, the South African–born inventor of PayPal and now the CEO of Tesla. There are some who believe he is heading for the mother of all (second-degree) failures. "Even by the standards of Silicon Valley," writes journalist Matthew DeBord, "what Tesla CEO Elon Musk is approaching would be failure on a whole new scale."[8] This refers to his production ambitions. In 2015, Tesla delivered 50,000 cars to as many people. Some time back, Tesla said that by 2020, they would be making half a million cars a year. Now they promise to have built that half a million by 2018.[9] Not all Tesla employees are loving this idea, and not everyone believes Elon Musk can reasonably deliver. But his motto is: "When something is important enough, you do it even if the odds are not in your favor."[10]

But if he fails, what's to lose? Money? He has plenty of that anyway, and he knows how to make it. "Failure on a whole new scale" is still just experimenting. If he succeeds, he will be an example of how to burn the midnight oil despite the naysayers. Potential failures like these are challenges set up by already massively successful individuals and companies. Google can play around in the same way; so can Microsoft and Apple. This is the realm of trying things out, and the secret is not being bothered by a less-than-ideal outcome—and not getting tired along the way.

This is the territory of "Never give up" and "If at first you don't succeed, try, try again." This actually has nothing to do with failure. Any failures along this road are not life-enders. The price paid for these failures is in time, money, and maybe pride—but not in human life.

Let's look at some of those endeavours and challenges in business, science, and technology where so-called failure can indeed be celebrated because each "failure" gets the participants one step closer to success. This is the realm where we're empowered: we set the goals; we decide how much is enough and when and if to call it quits. If we fail, nobody dies, nobody gets hurt. And let's be honest—"Fail Often; Fail Better" can be seen as the mantra of the privileged, those few who already know the taste of success in their fields—people not deterred by the results of their meandering experiments and the associated risk factors.

It's in science and technology that the myth of "Fail Often; Fail Better" emerges in all its glory. We've been convinced over the last century to trust the scientific method of enquiry as the gold standard for establishing the basis for any claims and assumptions. It's the realm, though, of trial and error. And it's *this* concept of failure that we might embrace and then rename, because these occurrences are simply not served by being termed "failures." These second-degree failures are explorations with numerous *unanticipated outcomes*. They are human adventures, and new and exciting things emerge from them that were never foreseen. Here, we see some real-world unexpected outcomes that are the results of trying to do something else. If we are fixated on the initial goals and desires of the companies pursuing them, these endeavours are "failures." If we focus on simply what happened as a result of this journey, we can marvel at the innovations, the discovery of things previously unimagined. Failure as a concept can be eliminated. If we learn how to fail brilliantly, we are, in fact, learning how to live brilliantly with unexpected outcomes.

One of the most well-known unanticipated drug-related outcomes happened in September 1928. After a summer holiday, Scottish biologist, botanist, and pharmacologist Alexander Fleming returned home and went into his lab in St. Mary's Hospital in London where he began a good old lab cleaning. He started with his petri dishes, in which he'd been cultivating *Staphylococcus* bacteria—the kind found in boils, abscesses, and other nasties. He'd forgotten to clean up properly, and a lump of mould had grown in the middle of a petri dish. Oddly, though, colonies of bacteria had grown everywhere *except* around the mould. He realized then that something was being produced by the mould that annihilated Staph bacteria. Later, that "something" was revealed to be a strain of *Penicillium notatum*, the first identified antibiotic. Thus the magic-bullet pill that prevented tens of thousands of deaths after D-Day was the result of an accident, an unintended outcome after failing to clean a petri dish.[11]

We can't make the assumption that effective drugs are the results of careful and meticulous planning, because all too frequently, they aren't. The invention of Viagra, for example, was also completely accidental.

The pharmaceutical company Pfizer was designing a drug (UK-92480) that they hoped would help relax blood vessels and mitigate the effects of angina, where blood flow to the heart is impeded by constricted vessels. Unfortunately, the drug wasn't working. Pfizer was all set to abandon future trials when men in the trials reported something unusual: frequent erections. Chris Wayman, Pfizer's senior scientist, discovered that when he placed the penile tissue of impotent men in a test tube and ran an electric current through it, nothing happened. But when he added the Viagra to the tissue, he saw "a restoration of the erectile response." And that, he said, meant he knew they were "onto something special."[12]

Pfizer released the drug in 1998. Since then, millions of men's lives have been changed. Success from failure, perhaps—but more accurately, an unanticipated outcome with positive results for many.

When we set ourselves up to hunt and capture success of any kind, we court the idea of personal failure. Once we set a goal and fix our eyes on the result, we lose the enormous potential that exists on any journey. There is a certain danger inherent in goal-setting, although we all believe that this is the great motivator that gets us moving through the world—striving, evolving.

If the destination is more important than the journey, and we focus on that, then our only destination is to reach the end of our lives, which isn't the reality. Our journey is and can be our destination, every step of the way. Each moment is an arrival. We expect things, anticipate them, wish for them. Sometimes they come; sometimes they don't. Most often, we have little control over the way the world works and the things that come our way—lucky or not.

The inventions of microwave ovens, X-rays, Velcro, and Scotchgard were all due to accidental discoveries. People were doing something completely different, and something happened that caught their attention. The stain- and water-resistant spray Scotchgard, for example, would not exist if it hadn't been for a lab assistant dropping a bottle of synthetic latex all over her tennis shoe. She was working under research chemist Patsy Sherman in 1952 on fluorochemicals. When they tried to remove the substance from the shoe, it wouldn't budge. The shoes remained white and looked exactly the same, but water, oil, and solvents did nothing to it. Scotchgard was on the shelves soon after.[13]

So what's the best way to think about second-degree failures? We know that we will be dealing with the results of intimate, personal, and maybe even internationally famous second-degree failures throughout our lives.

Here's a helpful thought: If we are stubbornly fixed on a goal, then we do not understand how life really works. Goals are excellent and important; they keep us moving and motivated. But if we instead remain as focused on our journey as on our destination, we have the opportunity to be enriched by our process. Even if we achieve our goal, human nature is such that it will not remain satisfied for long before we need to set a new goal and move towards that one. The idea of failure in these circumstances is narrow; it suggests that the only important thing is the end result, the net gain pitched against certain criteria. But we miss out on all the potential that lies scattered along the roadside of our journey. The only things we can actually know is that life is uncertain and that forces beyond our control will continue to shape us. The moral of the story is: if we remain open to the potential and don't beat ourselves (or others) up when we don't end up where we planned to go, we might discover subtle things along the way that have value we didn't anticipate discovering.

The ultimate goal of our lifetime is not the end of our lives. It is not how much stuff or how many achievements we have when we get there. The things that count are the experiences we have along the way. In the many books written on the "value of failure," there is a noble attempt to reassign a positive value to the word *failure*. The problem that we've already identified, though, is that the world does not work like that. The idea of failure is a societal negative. We do not, as a society, generally celebrate failure. If we work in sales, for example, or real estate, it's unimaginable that a boss would say, "I'm not concerned with you meeting your financial targets; the journey is as important as the destination." We will not be encouraged in most instances to fail. Our bosses will frown on material failure and will not cut us any slack. Failure to meet our goals most often results in justified stress: we may not have enough money to live on; we may lose our jobs to a more aggressive salesperson. The point is, we cannot control what comes to us. We can only control how we respond. We have to change our view of ourselves so that our personal journeys are not tied to the material outcome of our careers, our endeavours, and our strivings, and this is a magnificent challenge. Our bosses may threaten us with unemployment if we fail to meet our targets. We are explorers, like Shackleton—entrepreneurs of our own lives. We are trying things out. They may not work. There are adversarial forces out there, from bad weather to disastrous engineering to people who seem determined to make our lives difficult or challenging.

Our personal journeys have intrinsic value. We don't have to fail more, or better, or faster. If we want to be brilliant at failure, ironically, it makes more sense to consider erasing the word *failure* from how we think about ourselves and from the rich arena of human endeavour otherwise known as "life."

## BIG IDEAS

► Second-degree failures happen every day and are the results of any attempt or human endeavour to do anything.

► These failures are the unexpected outcomes we should expect.

► Once we set a goal and fix our eyes on the destination, we risk losing the enormous potential that exists on any journey.

► If we are tied to the results of our experiments, we will feel like failures if we don't get what we want.

► Our personal journeys have intrinsic value, regardless of the outcome.

## HELPFUL THOUGHTS ABOUT LIVING WITH SECOND-DEGREE FAILURES

► Understand that goals move constantly and that even if we achieve what we want today, tomorrow we will strive for something more.

► Think of each attempt to do something as an experiment.

► Accept that life is full of obstructions that will get in the way of goals.

► Separate the idea of personal failure from the outcome of the "experiment."

► Realise that life is much more like an explorer's journey than a race to the finish line. Live it brilliantly and fully without judging your endeavours as failures when they don't turn out the way you want them to.

## NOTES

1. Fuchs, Sir Vivian, and Sir Edmund Hillary. *The Crossing of Antarctica: The Commonwealth Trans-Antarctic Expedition 1955-1958*. London: Penguin, 1965.
2. Lovell, James A. "Houston, We've Had a Problem." *Apollo Expeditions to the Moon*, edited by Edgar M. Cortrite, chapter 13.2. Accessed February 22, 2017. https://history.nasa.gov/SP-350/toc.html.
3. Ibid.
4. Ibid., ch. 13.1.
5. Ibid., ch. 13.4.
6. Ibid., ch. 13.1.
7. DeBord, Matthew. "Elon Musk is setting himself up for an epic failure." *Business Insider Australia*, May 9, 2016. Accessed August 4, 2016. http://www.businessinsider.com.au/musk-epic-failure-2016-5?r=US&IR=T.
8. Ibid.
9. Ibid.
10. Pelley, Scott. "U. S., China, Russia, Elon Musk: Entrepreneur's 'insane' vision becomes reality." *CBS News*, May 22, 2012. http://www.cbsnews.com/news/us-china-russia-elon-musk-entrepreneurs-insane-vision-becomes-reality/.
11. *The Discovery and Development of Penicillin 1928–1945*. The American Chemical Society, 1999. Accessed August 18, 2016. https://www.acs.org/content/dam/acsorg/education/whatischemistry/landmarks/flemingpenicillin/the-discovery-and-development-of-penicillin-commemorative-booklet.pdf.
12. Jay, Emma. "Viagra and other drugs discovered by accident." *BBC News*, January 20, 2010. Accessed September 26, 2016. http://news.bbc.co.uk/2/hi/health/8466118.stm.

13. "Patsy Sherman: Invention of Scotchgard Stain Repellent." Women-inventors.com. Accessed October 10, 2016. http://www. women-inventors.com/Patsy-Sherman.asp.

## SUGGESTED READING

Breuning, Loretta Graziano. *Habits of a Happy Brain: Retrain Your Brain to Boost Your Serotonin, Dopamine, Oxytocin & Endorphin Levels*. Avon, MA: Adams Media, 2016.

*Antimicrobial Resistance: Tackling a Crisis for the Health and Wealth of Nations*. The Review on Antimicrobial Resistance, December 2014. https://amr-review.org/sites/default/files/AMR%20 Review%20Paper%20-%20Tackling%20a%20crisis%20for%20 the%20health%20and%20wealth%20of%20nations_1.pdf.

Robertson, Ian H. *The Winner Effect: The Neuroscience of Success and Failure*. New York: Thomas Dunne Books, 2012.

Sapolsky, Robert M. *Why Zebras Don't Get Ulcers: An Updated Guide to Stress, Stress-Related Diseases, and Coping*, 2nd Edition. New York: W. H. Freeman and Co., 1998.

# CHAPTER FOUR

# THIRD-DEGREE FAILURES AND THEIR ARBITRARY NATURE

**F**ailure is a term that we use every day. We fling it around and believe in its existence as a singular concept without question. In a world driven crazy by the obsession with monetary success, failure conjures up images of that ultimate loser, the one who never makes it. In contrast to that is a recent explosion of literature telling us that really, failure is a good thing—that if you're not failing, you're not engaging. It's a noble attempt to save us from our own illusions, but it's not very effective, and here's why: no matter how many times we might be told by prominent entrepreneurs and perhaps even educators to embrace failure, to fail more often, to fail better, the reality is that society still frowns on failures. From our education systems to our legal systems to our medical systems, we are on an A-to-F scale. Getting an F is a bad grade. You fail.

We have built our world on the neurobiology that propels us forward, that creates winners and losers, and so "failing better" is just a euphemism for "try again, harder next time." It doesn't mean "deliberately ruin your attempts over and over." So even the idea of "failing brilliantly" is a contradiction in terms.

We still collect and collate all failures under one umbrella, and in most aspects of our lives, we don't treat this lump of unanticipated outcomes as a good thing, regardless of what the books say. Life is like this: *things don't go according to plan.* Having failure as a term to throw over those things that don't go according to plan is especially damaging in the area of what we've termed "third-degree failures." These are the ones *we* create entirely.

The only thing we learn from failing, writes Alfie Kohn in "The Failure of Failure," is that we don't like it and don't want to repeat the experience. The idea of productive failure, he argues, is a residue of the protestant work ethic where suffering is somehow mandatory on the pathway to achieving desired goals: "The benefits of screwing up are wildly overrated. What's most reliably associated with successful outcomes, it turns out, are prior experiences with success, not with failure."[1] And that is because, regardless of all the hype around the benefits of failure as a precursor to success, society judges failures harshly, puts all kinds of failures into one basket.

This is unfortunate, because in a myriad of ways, third-degree failures give rise to spectacular discoveries and revelations that are *not* failures in themselves. Again, the original goal isn't achieved, but new knowledge, new ideas, new discoveries entirely unanticipated come to the fore. If second-degree failures are those large-scale "failures" that lead to new ideas and discoveries, third-degree failures are personal and almost always arbitrary failures we invent for ourselves. We learn to use second-degree failures as stepping stones to success; third-degree failures are false notions we need to break.

Our obsession with material progress is *not* the recipe for us living longer, healthier lives. It is much more complex than this. It's how we feel and how we respond to events that becomes important. But we have wired those two together as if this is so. Some of the people on the planet living the longest and possibly happiest lives are the rural folk of Okinawa, Japan, and the Mediterranean island of Sardinia.[2] They eat exceptionally well, work physically hard, and have a sense of community and purpose. That word *purpose* is what we're missing in our success-obsessed society. Our purpose is too often getting a high grade, making money, or collecting stuff, which we tie to our ultimate survival. And while there is some value to having enough to survive, the stuff itself is not the kind of purpose that brings us long-lasting happiness or long life.

So when we talk of success, we're talking about a narrow definition of success, and we could, with a simple thought, redefine that—and, by association, failure.

In our quest for progress and success, we've invented this thing called "failure," which in most circumstances does not give us what we want: health, happiness, long life. Someone in the United States who ties his life's purpose to getting as much stuff and fame and fortune and wealth as possible could die at forty-two of a heart attack, while a hardworking farmer in Sardinia with few possessions who enjoys his life's journey, enjoys his friends, and has a sense of purpose could live until 102.[3]

The most important thing is that third-degree failures are an epidemic of the modern industrialised world. We can be bold about our approach to them. What would happen, for example, if we removed the word *failure* from all third-degree fails and replaced it with the words *unanticipated outcome*? Would that change anything? Certainly for second-degree failures such as the Apollo 13 mission and Shackleton's Voyage, the outcomes were excellent, if *entirely unanticipated*. The knowledge they gained through the experience—the innovations, the collaborations—all of those human experiences were unantici-pated outcomes of these particular missions.

And importantly, this would be true for third-degree failures too.

# EDUCATION AND FAILURE

Education is a classic example of where these so-called failures play themselves out in the lives of children and young people every single day.

Putting failures into categories and then redefining what failure means in that context may take us as a society towards a new mindset—a new paradigm—and could lead to positive results in many areas that affect how happy we are and, impor-tantly, how long we live.

Understanding this, some schools and institutes of higher learning have eliminated the traditional grading system. This works at a fundamental level for children especially, because they develop according to markers that don't set them up as if they are running a race. There are no winners and no losers, just journeyers, people climbing different mountains, finding differ-ent pathways towards their destinations. In school settings, we can embrace trial and error and be unafraid of the outcome if it's not loaded or graded according to pass/fail criteria. If we use a trial-and-error approach, a progressive journey approach in every single subject in every grade, we allow for the true nature of people to express itself. We can use the scientific method: *Try pointing the steam vent at this angle to make the turbine turn, and if it doesn't work, we try other angles until we find the opti-mum position.* None of these points along the journey are then failures; they're just experiments. *This angle doesn't work at all; this one works, but not as well as the final one.*

It's the same with essays: *This essay makes a few good points, but the language could be more sophisticated and you could discuss how growing up in the war influenced the writer's choice of subject matter. This is for the next draft.* No grades, just the idea that when you've done that, you can move on to the next level, the next assignment, because you have all the grounding you need. You get to compete with yourself, with others if you want, but you don't ever wear the label "Failure" or "D student" on your head or in your heart. And no one tells you to embrace failure, because there is not failure. Like climbing a mountain, there are just different levels, and when you're super fit and the conditions are right, you reach the summit, if that is your goal. This approach builds resilience in children whose neural pathways are developing at a rapid rate. If we don't instil feelings of unworthiness in our children from an early age, it will lead to them feeling less "poor," less "subordinate." And maybe that extends their lives and ours. If we could erase the word and concept of *failure* from third-degree failures entirely, we would eventually affect our individual neural patterning and the responses of society. Our ideas of failure need to become more sophisticated if we want to change our lives in a positive way.

This could be a typical scenario: imagine two Australian eighteen-year-olds, Justin and Mark. Their final English exam has a pass mark of 50 percent. Justin ends up getting 48 percent, and so he fails the entire exam and has to retake it. Justin is now in the same boat as Mark, who didn't even study and got 10 percent on the exam—yet, clearly, Justin knows most of his stuff. Justin now feels like a failure. In the next exam, which is literature, the pass mark is set at 40 percent. Getting 48 percent for that exam would be a healthy pass mark, and when Justin gets that mark, he feels elated; he knows what he needs to know to not have to retake the test, even though he got the same percentage of answers wrong as he did on the previous exam. Of course, at some point, the education or teaching authorities made a decision that in order to pass English Language, 50 percent of the questions have to be right whilst all the other exams have 40 percent as a pass mark. It is potentially arbitrary, but the feelings of failure that Justin has after failing English Language dog him for months, though he got only a single question wrong and is otherwise a competent student. If he retook the test immediately afterwards, chances are he might easily get the 50 percent required, as multiple choice tests are notorious for being a snapshot of a single moment in a student's day and results can vary considerably.[4]

At a nearby university, however, Rachel is doing her doctorate. When she submits her thesis, she gets one of three responses: either it is accepted, it is accepted provided she makes minor changes, or it will be accepted once she makes major changes. She is deemed either competent or on the way to becoming competent. She is never given a grade, and she has the opportunity to take the time she needs to get through the examination process. Could schools and universities and the entire educational industry work like this? Would they be successful? Of course. There are plenty of examples that we'll get to later, but most of us are caught up in a world where kids are graded from the minute they start school, and our brains are wired from early on to respond to the cues we are given as to whether we are "successes" or "failures." Our bodies respond accordingly. When we get an A on a test, we have surges of dopamine and testosterone and we feel we are winning in the great competition of life. Yet this structure is completely arbitrary, made by us, and does not necessarily translate into the things we think are connected to these early grades: later financial success, happiness, and health. Educators (fallible human beings), not God or the universe, make up the pass marks. Then they decide that this is an A, or a B, or a C, or that a pass mark for this assignment is 40 percent while for another it may be 33.3 percent. As a result, a whole section of the population walks around carrying the idea of themselves as failures like an invisible malady.

Charlie is seven years old and he still can't read. Most of his classmates are reading by now, yet he struggles to just remember whether he is looking at a B or a D and what sound it should make. He can't ever remember how the words are spelled.

After a year or two of failing small tests, Charlie's brain is already wired so that he fears tests and thinks of himself as stupid, a failure. He will carry that perception of himself right up into high school and perhaps even into the world of university and work, because he is now part of a group of children who are always behind, always failing, even if the reason is that brains develop at vastly different rates—and that children become proficient at things in such a staggered way that at any given time, there is a full six-year gap in the capabilities of the least and most proficient students in the class.

But perhaps Charlie ends up going to Sanborn Regional High School in New Hampshire, one of many schools focusing on competency-based education.[5] They have done away with letter grades. Teachers give students extensive and helpful feedback, and students are given a "formative expectations checklist" to self-assess their assignments before they hand them in. Students are involved in projects that take place within a flexible schedule. So how would Charlie's report card at Sanborn look? It looks nothing like his previous report card of Cs, Ds, and Fs. It shows a list of key competencies and then states whether Charlie is proficient in that competency or not yet. If he doesn't yet show competency, he can do things to get "recovery" credit. And he's kind of surprised, because he is proficient in most of his subjects. He is encouraged, given the time during the term to reach the level of understanding required to make him competent. There is a whole system set up to support him in areas where he needs help. At the end, his competencies are translated into a GPA and end up as his final grade.[6]

Many colleges and universities across the United States have taken this approach on board, but it is still the exception rather than the rule.[7] New College in Florida, Evergreen State College in Washington state, and Reed College in Oregon offer competency-based degrees in all areas of study. You work until you are competent; you fulfil tasks and hand in a senior project to demonstrate your learning. No project does not mean a failure. It just means no project. This is a very different approach. You are not being graded and judged; you are given feedback and agency without the stigma attached, which goes to show that our concept of academic failure is based on a completely arbitrary and unnecessary paradigm. Third-degree failures are the result of our own random constructions.

Grades do three things, according to Alfie Kohn:

▶ *Grades tend to diminish students' interest in whatever they're learning.* A "grading orientation" and a "learning orientation" have been shown to be inversely related—every study that has ever investigated the impact on intrinsic motivation of receiving grades . . . has found a negative effect.

▶ *Grades create a preference for the easiest possible task.* . . . [Students are] responding to adults who, by telling them the goal is to get a good mark, have sent the message that success matters more than learning.

▶ *Grades tend to reduce the quality of students' thinking.* . . . In one experiment, students told they'd be graded on how well they learned a social studies lesson had more trouble understanding the main point of the text than did students who were told that no grades would be involved. Even on a measure of rote recall, the graded group remembered fewer facts a week later.[8]

In a recent article discussing some of the main issues with school assessment in Australia, Professor Geoff Masters, CEO of the Australian Council for Educational Research—a body that provides assessment resources to schools and advice to governments—writes:

There is a major flaw in the way we currently assess school students. By labelling them as either "good" or "poor" learners based on their overall grades at the end of each year, students have no clear idea whether they are making progress over extended periods of time. A student who receives a D this year, a D next year, and a D the year after . . . may conclude that there is something stable about their ability to learn (they are a "D student"). Many of these students eventually disengage from the schooling process.[9]

Masters maintains that a shift is needed to reflect progress over time as kids journey through school. This would be more valuable than the As and Fs that await thousands of youngsters in their report cards at the end of the year and lead to countless young people viewing themselves as "failures."

Of course, there are students who, even with competency-based learning, never succeed and, even with time, never get better at reading or math. These students are not failures. They often fall outside the academic ladder criteria and have gifts in areas that aren't assessed in the classroom. To take away the stigma of "failure" may help these students too. When we eliminate grades, we take away the accompanying loads of shame and the race to the top and the fear of failure. There is no top. There is just a journey, a task. Those students who do not meet the proficiency standards initially should be given all the assistance and opportunities to move themselves forward. Of course, it depends on the student. Someone who does not provide any evidence for academic feedback or assessment may in fact have other gifts that would be better pursued elsewhere. It is then up to the teachers and support staff to identify pathways where those students may shine in their own right.

Shelley Davidow, the coauthor of this book, has helped many talented but academically "failing" youngsters to find alternatives to traditional schooling, such as the pursuit of non-academic courses that build skills and capacities in specialised areas. One of her biggest academic "failures" was a budding musician who submitted no academic work at all in tenth grade. Shelley encouraged him to pursue a vocational training in music technology. He got into recording and now makes his living as a musician. Another such academic "failure" did an apprenticeship in construction and is now outearning all of his old teachers. These kids are not failures; they just weren't academically-minded or -driven. And our modern world needs more than a population of Einsteins.

We are caught in this myth of academic failure—"Good grades in school mean better opportunities to get into a good college, which means more opportunity to get a good job, which means a better opportunity to be financially successful, which means eventual happiness"—and it's time to explode it. In fact, even just in terms of financial wealth and success, the equation doesn't add up.

In *The Millionaire Mind* by Thomas Stanley, a Harvard-trained mathematician reveals in his study that there was no correlation between school success and later financial success. Grades, SAT scores, whether or not the students were valedictorians—none of that mattered. In fact, some of the richest people in the United States were dropouts. Academic success is not a predictor of future millionaire status.[10]

In addition, Karen Arnold, professor of education at Boston University, states:

"To know that a person is a valedictorian is to only know that he or she is exceedingly good at achievement as measured by grades. It tells you nothing about how they react to the vicissitudes of life."[11]

## CONTEXT AND THIRD-DEGREE FAILURES

Every day, we have many chances to fail, and society makes it hard for us to erase the idea of personal failure from our lives. But although the experience of "failing" is real, that failure is always relative, and there are ways to reimagine failure so that we can dissolve it in our own personal universe.

Here's an example of how our feelings of failure are tied intricately to context and perception: if we went onto a game show, picked a winning ticket out of a hat, won ten thousand dollars, and walked away with that, we'd feel great. We'd be ten thousand dollars richer than we were yesterday, and that would make us happy. But if we were playing for the chance to win one hundred thousand dollars and we got only ten thousand dollars, chances are we'd suffer feelings of failure and loss, though we never had the one hundred thousand in the first place. Our concepts of failure are circumstantial and often don't relate to the reality we're confronted with. In the first scenario, we are ten thousand dollars richer. In the second scenario, we are still ten thousand dollars richer. But in the first, we feel elated, successful, like winners, and in the second, we feel deflated, failed, like losers. Our concept of failure is entirely dependent on how we write the script.

In *Thinking, Fast and Slow*, Daniel Kahneman discusses this tendency of ours and highlights how we are primed for certain behaviours. The contextual nature of our feelings of loss or dissatisfaction are just that—contextual. Loss aversion motivates us to do weird things. When we act out of our fear of loss, we are likely to overspend on a house or be upset even if we win something big because we wanted to win something even bigger.[12]

Our concept of failure is a deeply personal thing. What seems to be a failure for one person will be a success for another. Imagine two people in vastly different circumstances: Tom, who has been in a coma for eight weeks, finally manages to walk six feet across the room. This is a milestone, a huge success. Sally, who failed to reach the summit of Mt. Everest on a recent adventure to Nepal, feels like a failure. Sally would think nothing of Tom's achievement, while Tom would hardly view Sally climbing Mt. Everest but not reaching the summit as a failure.

Janice Bridges[13] is a friend who has been diagnosed with cancer twice. The last time she had it, she was in a coma and everyone had come to say goodbye. She was given hours to live, and her family, including her two teenage children, was at her bedside to be there with her in her final moments. That happened five years ago. She made a miraculous recovery and came back quite literally from the jaws of death. A few months ago, she found a lump in her breast and had her third diagnosis. The cancer, her oncologist told her, was stage I, contained, and not a metastatic version of the previous cancer. When she went in for surgery, the doctors got it all. She began the road to recovery once more, full of positive energy. Luckily, she said, she got the "good cancer" this time. Having almost died five years ago, she looked at this third diagnosis and saw it, incredibly, as a surmountable challenge rather than a death sentence. Now imagine how different the reaction to a diagnosis of stage I breast cancer might be to a woman who has been healthy her entire life and has never been through Janice's struggles. Failure is relative.

If we understand that failures are not these objective things that happen to us when we do things wrong, we might be able to realise that we are constantly being set up by others and by ourselves. We contextualise and compare ourselves to others, to our expectations and desires, and we mark ourselves according to those constantly changing expectations, thinking the marks are permanent.

The first noble truth, according to Buddha over two and a half thousand years ago, was that life would inevitably fail to live up to our expectations of it and that much of our suffering was because of desires we could not fulfil, goals we could not achieve. He maintained, though, that even when we satisfied our immediate wants, the satisfaction would not last and we would keep wanting more—and it's hard not to say that everywhere we look today, this appears to be true. The remedy he gave was to practise not being attached to stuff, to our desires. In that way, he said, we could alleviate our suffering. We'll delve into this more in Chapter Nine, where we discuss philosophical and religious worldviews as solutions for dealing with failure.

Leo Goldberg[14] is a businessman in California who recently lost his business after almost thirty years of hard work. His partner had made some terrible decisions without his knowledge. Legal costs as he fought the inevitable left him with no option but to acknowledge that his dream of eventually being able to retire on the basis of all his hard work had completely vanished.

After being his own boss for so many years, he had to begin looking for a job. He became a salaried employee, earning enough to survive but facing the fact that he, at age sixty, would likely be working for the rest of his life. No retirement, no nest egg. Everything had been in the business.

Those of us who knew him were worried about him. Would he cope? We knew that he had worked seventeen-hour days for his entire working life, most often six days a week, and all of that had come to this.

But Leo had an interesting attitude. When we spoke to him over dinner one evening and asked him how he was doing and what he thought of all this, he smiled and shrugged his shoulders. "That's life, guys," he said. "Sure, it was tough and I had my moments, but in the end, what could I do about it? I have a job, I'm enjoying my weekends. Life's too short to let this stuff bring you down. I had to change my plans, change my dreams, but I'm still here, I'm alive. That's what counts."

We could imagine that he would want to rage against the unfairness of the situation, to want revenge on the partner who did so much damage, who effectively ruined his life.

But he didn't see it that way.

Losing his business in this way was a very unpleasant, unwanted, and unexpected outcome. Leo acknowledged this, and then he put all his energy into remaking his life, finding joy in the things he liked to do and not tying his own sense of self to what happened. He could not ever get back what was lost, yet he did not feel like a failure. His choice was to look at it this way: he understood that he had set himself goals, and then life threw stuff at him over which he had little control. He said: *You just have to get on with it.* It wasn't that he wasn't attached to his life's work, his dreams. He just knew that there was nothing to be done except to live each day and make the most of what he had.

Another area where we judge ourselves and are judged by others is in our personal relationships. Society sets up norms and expectations, and then we "pass" or "fail" at them. But this is just another grading system. It is just a construct.

When we go into a relationship and eventually get married, we somehow blindly accept this equation: staying married equals success; divorce equals failure. These are narrow parameters, and even though we know this is intrinsically not true—that for many people, staying in a relationship is far worse than getting out of it—we are so often still tied by the expectations of those around us.

Lara James[15] is a culinary producer on a well-known cooking show in Los Angeles who was thirty-three when the man she was dating asked her to marry him. She was getting to a stage where all her friends were getting married and having kids, and there was enormous pressure for her to do the same. So she took the step she thought she needed to when he asked her. She said, "He was a guy who was not present. I was so flattered he asked me to marry him, and I thought I could help him become more present, more rooted."

Two months later, her grandfather died and she went to the East Coast to be with her family. Her husband declined to come, and she felt he wasn't present again and did not care about her loss. That night, something happened.

> It was a weird night. I went to bed early. I woke up in such a state at 11:30 p.m., and it was as if my grand-father was there in the room. I felt he was saying that something was wrong. There was this presence of: *You*

*need to wake up. This isn't your life.* I couldn't sleep. My heart was racing. Only later did I find out that that night, my husband cheated on me while I was out of town. Months later, he told me what he had done and was convinced I wouldn't leave him. He thought that I would view leaving him or divorcing him as a failure—that I was so idealistic that I wouldn't leave even if he did terrible things. It took me a few months to get my head around it and realise this situation wasn't for me. It was as if my grandfather had told me not to be so sacrificial. But at the time, it felt like such a failure . . . I wondered how I could have been so shortsighted—I was bowing to all this pressure—there I was at thirty-four and there's this pressure to have it all figured out. For women, leaving a relationship doesn't seem to be as accepted as part of our culture as readily as it is for a man. I did not see my marriage failing like this . . . but in the end, here's what happened: I realised that my fear of failing was bigger than my actual happiness. That was my biggest lesson. In the aftermath of that "failed" marriage, I made res-olutions like *I'm not even going to date till I'm fifty* or *I'm not going to be with anybody again.* I was just too scared to see the relationship for what it was.

Lara had been sucked in by flattery; the romantic idealism that she could help her husband had propelled her into an untenable situation.

It was the same as being seduced by an amazing job offer, but when you think about day in, day out and consider whether this will this fill you up and bring you joy and emotional well-being, maybe it isn't so great after all. We get so clouded by the seduction of outside stuff. That protection device, closing myself off, not dat-ing until I was fifty—now *that* could have been failure.

Because ultimately what did happen was that love came in the side door in a pure, amazing form when I was not interested or looking. I am now so happy and grateful. I'm with a wonderful person, and I'm grateful for what happened, because I can see now very clearly how leaving that marriage was not a failure. It's amazing to me what we'll do to avoid the idea of failure even if we know it's an unhappy path.

If life, including marriage, is a journey—and it surely is, as we're trying out new things every day—then we should know that unexpected outcomes are highly possible.

# SHIFTING GOALPOSTS

The only thing we can be sure of in this world is that change is inevitable and that we are part of that change. Goals move. Intentions shift. Even if we get what we aim for, we will soon have new aims and new desires.

Our third-degree failures are imposed on us by ourselves and by our society, by bosses demanding we meet targets, by educators demanding our children meet standards.

Recently, at the University of the Sunshine Coast in Queensland, Australia, in a creative writing class which focused on introducing students to the publishing industry, the question was asked of twenty-two students and a visiting author: *At which point will you think of yourself as a successful writer?*

Student one answered, "When I finish writing my current manuscript."

Student two: "When my novel is accepted."

Student three: "When I find my book on the shelf in a major bookstore."

The teacher: "When I'm living off my writing without needing to supplement it by teaching to survive."

And finally, the visiting author: "When I have sold the movie deal for my book, have a few million dollars in the bank, and am sitting on a beach in Thailand sipping cocktails."

So, failure for student one is that she never finishes her manuscript.

Failure for student two is that her novel is never accepted.

Failure for student three is that he doesn't find his book on the shelf in a major bookstore.

The teacher's failure is that he never makes a living from his writing.

The visiting author's failure is that he never sells the movie rights for his book, nor does he make several million dollars, nor does he arrive in Thailand to drink to those successes.

Failure in this context is remarkably different from person to person—and, more importantly, these students' ideas of failure will likely evolve as they progress. The student who finishes her manuscript will then want to get it published; the student who gets her novel published will not feel really successful until she wins an award, and on and on. And this is because, at the root of it, it is an evolutionary human trait to aspire, to ascend, to achieve, and so we need to be hyperaware that the definition of what constitutes failure in our lives is constantly shifting. If we are going to fail, then why not fail brilliantly?

Ideally, schools and universities would eventually erase the entire concept of failure from their domains. The CEO of a real estate company would focus on affirming the potential of an underperforming agent and providing strategies for improvement that would not suggest that the person herself is a failure. But this utopian state of affairs is not likely to happen anytime soon. So we, as free-thinking individuals with the power to write our own responses and stories, have to take matters into our own hands. We can't control what the world does, but we can control how we respond to these so-called third-degree failures.

So how do we take action to protect ourselves from falling victim to the idea of personal failure when the world is so relentlessly dividing us into two camps: successes and failures?

We start with looking at the unpleasant things in life as an assignment. Let's imagine a worst-case scenario:

You work as a real estate agent, and your job requires that you meet your target of getting thirty leads per day—and you can't change that. The boss puts pressure on everyone and has a porcupine personality. She constantly favours your successful colleague whose sales are through the roof and frowns on your comparative failure. What choice do you have?

You can leave. But you might not be able to find other employment quickly enough.

You can stay and take on the idea of yourself as a failure, beating yourself up at your inadequacies, and embracing the perception that you are useless.

Or you can begin to look for another job where the company ethics match your own. In the meantime, you have a choice to not take on the perception that you, personally, are a failure. Your ability to get leads is no reflection of who you are as a person. If you walked into a completely different job tomorrow, this issue would not follow you. Therefore, you have total freedom to refrain from buying into the idea that you are a failure. Getting the leads is not the point of life. Learning to deal with the porcupine boss, believing in yourself when she is tearing you down, and looking for a better job . . . this is the point of life. Using this situation to grow strong and resilient is now your new assignment, even as you continue to bring in a miserable amount of leads.

When we're able to do this, to walk away from situations without fearing some external judgement about failure, then we are finding our way to manage the unwanted outcomes of a situation. We are freeing ourselves from the definitions of "failure" that society imposes on us. We liberate ourselves to live our lives outside of the criteria of success and failure. And though it is a tough journey, because it's stressful and we don't know what the outcome will be, it has the possibility of showing us who we really are—and we don't need thirty leads a day to tell us that we are valuable as human beings.

## BIG IDEAS

- ► We construct the parameters of third-degree failures.
- ► Third-degree failures are arbitrary in nature.
- ► Feelings of failure are tied to context and perception.
- ► We often pay a high emotional price for being deemed a failure.
- ► The power of these failures fades the minute we shift our thinking from *I'm a failure* to *I have not met certain professional/personal goals, but I am not a failure as a person.*

## HELPFUL THOUGHTS ABOUT LIVING WITH THIRD-DEGREE FAILURES

- ► Reject the perception that you are a failure—this is empowering and aligns with the idea that your personal worth is not tied to grades, earnings, or outcomes that are imposed on you.
- ► Think yourself free of the values that trap people between two illusory concepts (success and failure), and liberate yourself to live outside narrow definitions.
- ► Spend time with people who value the qualities that are truly yours. Change the way you talk about yourself and avoid negative comments about yourself.
- ► Keep a book in which you write down every compliment or affirmative positive thing people say about you. Look at this often.

## NOTES

1. Kohn, Alfie. "The Failure of Failure." *Huffington Post*, June 23, 2016. Accessed February 26, 2017. http://www.huffingtonpost.com/alfie-kohn/the-failure-of-failure_b_10635942.html.

2. Buettner, Dan. *The Blue Zone: Lessons for Living Longer from the People Who've Lived the Longest*. Washington, DC: National Geographic, 2008.

3. Poulain, Michel, Gianni Pes, and Luisa Salaris. "A Population Where Men Live as Long as Women: Villagrande Strisaili, Sardinia." *Journal of Aging Research* (2011): 153756. https://www.ncbi.nlm.nih.gov/pmc/articles/PMC3205712/.

4. Strauss, Valerie. "The real problem with multiple-choice tests." Washington Post, January 25, 2013. https://www.washingtonpost.com/news/answer-sheet/wp/2013/01/25/the-real-problem-with-multiple-choice-tests/?utm_term=.5f2df75fb240.

5. Nelson, Sharleen. "New Hampshire Schools Roll Out Competency-Based Learning Model." *The Journal*, January 23, 2013. Accessed February 26, 2017. https://thejournal.com/articles/2013/01/23/new-hampshire-schools-roll-out-competency-based-learning-model.aspx.

6. Sturgis, Chris. "Raising the Bar at Sanborn Regional High School." Competency Works, March 19, 2014. Accessed February 25, 2017. http://www.competencyworks.org/understanding-competency-education/6269/.

7. Noe-Payne, Mallory. "No grades, no problem: How one high school is transforming learning." WGBH News, June 18, 2015. Accessed March 14, 2017. http://www.pri.org/stories/2015-06-18/no-grades-no-problem-how-one-high-school-transforming-learning.

8. Kohn, Alfie. "The Case Against Grades." Educational Leadership, November 2011. Accessed March 14, 2017. http://www.alfiekohn.org/article/case-grades/.

9. Masters, Geoff. "Rethinking how we assess learning in schools." The Conversation, February 6, 2017. Accessed March 14, 2017. http://www.theconversation.com/rethinking-how-we-assess-learning-in-schools-71219.

10. Stanley, Thomas J. *The Millionaire Mind*. Kansas City: Andrews McMeel Publishing, 2001.

11. Johnson, Steve, and Matt Murray. "Valedictorians Stay Levelheaded about Being No. 1." *Chicago Tribune*, May 29, 1992. Accessed March 14, 2017. http://articles.chicagotribune.com/ 1992-05-29/news/ 9202170890_1_salutatorians-valedictorians-study.

12. Kahneman, Daniel. *Thinking, Fast and Slow*. New York: Farrar, Straus and Giroux, 2013.

13. Janice Bridges. Interview with the authors, December 2016. Name changed for privacy.

14. Leo Goldberg. Interview with the authors, January 2017. Name changed for privacy.

15. Lara James. Interview with the authors, December 2016. Name changed for privacy.

# CHAPTER FIVE

# FAMOUS AND SUCCESSFUL PEOPLE—AND THE MYTH OF FAILURE

Here are many extraordinarily famous and materially successful people who have a lot to say about failure. In a TED talk entitled "The Failurist," Markus Zusak, bestselling author of *The Book Thief*, said, "Failure has been my best friend as a writer. It tests you to see if you have what it takes to see it through." He sees failure as the thing that pushes us along, once we acknowledge it. "It's overcoming our insecurities and fears that makes us stronger and better, and it's what gives success meaning."[1] He maintains that we can't succeed all the time and that failure is a good teacher. But he makes this statement from a position of financial, material, and artistic success.

Celebrities are often heard giving inspirational talks on failure, and not least of these is J. K. Rowling, world-famous author of the Harry Potter series. She gave what was possibly one of the most well-known speeches on failure. She addressed a hall full of Harvard graduates in a commencement speech in 2008 and reflected on her life and the complete failure that she maintains she once was:

> Ultimately, we all have to decide for ourselves what constitutes failure, but the world is quite eager to give you a set of criteria if you let it. So I think it fair to say that by any conventional measure, a mere seven years after my graduation day, I had failed on an epic scale. An exceptionally short-lived marriage had imploded, and I was jobless, a lone parent, and as poor as it is possible to be in modern Britain without being homeless. The fears that my parents had had for me, and that I had had for myself, had both come to pass, and by every usual standard, I was the biggest failure I knew.
>
> Now, I am not going to stand here and tell you that failure is fun. That period of my life was a dark one, and I had no idea that there was going to be what the press has since represented as a kind of fairy-tale resolution. I had no idea then how far the tunnel extended, and for a long time, any light at the end of it was a hope rather than a reality.[2]

Entrepreneur Richard Branson, founder of the Virgin Group, writes:

> I've been failing for as long as I can remember. In fact, I've been failing even longer than that—I fell over many times as a baby before learning how to walk. The pattern has continued into adulthood and my life as an entrepreneur, and I have learned and loved every step of the way.[3]

We've already talked about billionaire Elon Musk, who at the time of writing has a net worth of around twelve billion dollars.

He has perfected the art of what he terms "failing successfully." Musk was born in South Africa in 1971. His dad was an engineer and his mom a model. As a child, he loved books and was withdrawn and shy; as a result, he found himself horribly bullied at school. He doesn't look back on those days with any relish. But when he moved to Canada at the age of seventeen, things began to change for him. He started playing around seriously with technology and eventually went into business with his brother, founding the company Zip2, an online version of The Yellow Pages.

A parallel entrepreneur (investing in more than one idea at a time), he has been on a knife edge several times over. He has been kicked out of his own position as CEO of the companies he founded on at least two occasions. He was removed by the board of directors from Zip2 because they thought him too inexperienced to take the company into the future. He did manage to hang onto his shares, though, and made $22 million when the company finally sold. He was dumped from PayPal, which he founded, and his later investments in Tesla and SpaceX have spent time teetering on the edge of total financial dissolution before making it over the hurdles. SpaceX was saved at the last moment with the successful launch of the first privately funded, reusable liquid fuel rocket in 2008 and made itself even more futureproof by adding the first privately funded successful space flight to the International Space Station to its list of achievements in 2012. NASA ultimately invested billions in SpaceX, saving Musk and the company from ruin and putting him at the forefront of innovative-genius success. His disasters and potential disasters culminating in such overwhelming successes have only fuelled his ambitions and led to more innovation and success, which is why he's not risk averse to any new adventures that may seem impossible dreams to the eyes of a common onlooker.[4]

As a result, his thoughts about failure are interesting and are evidently the words by which he seems to live: "If something is important enough, even if the odds are against you, you should still do it." Or: "Failing is an option here. If you aren't failing, you aren't innovating enough."[5]

# VIEWING FAILURE FROM A POSITION OF MATERIAL SUCCESS

These quotes on failure are designed to be inspirational, to motivate the rest of us, to make us feel better about the million things in life that don't pan out as we wish them to. Yet look at these people speaking on failure. They are, according to the criteria of financial, social, and material status, the epitome of success: they are brilliant, they are wealthy, and they are world famous. They come at the concept of failure from a position of extraordinary distinction. Their material successes are the results of a combination of brilliance, tenacity, and good fortune, according to extensive research by Malcolm Gladwell in his book *Outliers*.[6] And one cannot deny that for these people, their "failures" *are* incredibly valuable as the means to an end. Their so-called failures have simply been steps along the road to success—and so they are making sense of these failures in the context of and from the position of quite exceptional privilege.

If J. K. Rowling had given up after twelve publishers rejected *Harry Potter*, if Markus Zusak had remained a mid-list author with a five-hundred-page manuscript gathering dust and rejections under his bed, if Sir Richard Branson had not overcome some of the hurdles in his way, if Elon Musk had never made it out of South Africa—would these famous individuals be saying the same things about failure? We would never know, because unless you have "made it," no one is going to listen. Fame and fortune give people the platform to be heard and seen. We are interested in the so-called failures of these wildly successful people because of their astronomical success, and because we think that maybe they have a formula we can apply to our own lives. We think that imitating certain behaviours and approaches might lead to our own success, lift us out of a mediocre existence, and give us the chance to be a member of that very small elite. If these individuals weren't successful, we wouldn't know them, we wouldn't have a reason to hang onto their words, and we wouldn't be interested in what they had to say about failure.

This is not an undermining of J. K. Rowling's struggle by any means, but the fact is, being a poor single mother on welfare in the U. K. is a fate shared by hundreds of thousands. It seems that her words about failure then condemn all those women and all of us to thinking that these lives of struggle are failures unless they eventuate in billionaire author status![7, 8] This is not going to happen to the majority of those people—she's one in a million. So when we are motivated by her failure speech, we end up lending weight to the burden that we all carry when we don't "make it." We buy into the failure-success dichotomy and make it hard for millions of us to value our struggles—not because they ultimately lead to success but because they shape us. We are led to believe that a life without riches has less value than a life defined by enormous wealth. So in light of J. K. Rowling's success, she sees her normal and unremarkable life before the Harry Potter series as a spectacular fail. And as the rest of the population searches for role models and heroes, they hang on to these success stories as metaphors. *She was poor once*, we think. *She was a failure. Now she's ultra-wealthy. That could be me.* Chances are, though, it may very well not be. And then what? Is the rest of the population then just doomed to seeing their lives as failures?

The point is, if they had not been wildly successful, these folks would not have been noticed. And though we listen to them speak about failure and hold them up as examples of what we can do and be, we have to know that when they talk about failure, they are not really talking about failure at all; they are, to quote Thomas Edison, talking about the "ten thousand" ways things didn't work out until, of course, they did.[9]

The message is that as long as we are alive and breathing, we cannot know, even if we think we have failed, whether the very next step will be the hard-earned success that makes all the preceding stumbles make sense. And if the journey doesn't lead to the planned destination—if, like Shackleton's expedition and the Apollo 13 mission, we miss the mark but survive—we can't devalue our lives or lose our sense of purpose just because we don't match up to the image of societal success.

Failure as seen by Rowling, Branson, Zusak, and Musk is not the failure of most ordinary people. Until each of those people succeeded, sure, they experienced setbacks, unanticipated outcomes, and disappointments, which in retrospect they can say were the stepping stones to their eventual successes. But they did not struggle for long; all of them were rich and powerful by the time they were in their thirties. They did not fight uphill battles for survival their whole lives. They did not exhaust themselves or have long enough without rewards to subject them to the loser effect. What they term "failures" sits more honestly under the term "challenges"—which they overcame quickly and spectacularly.

# BUSTING THE MYTH OF SUCCESS

The American dream is based on the philosophy that you can do anything if you put your mind to it. But so many people put their minds to it and don't manage to get where they are aiming to go. Plenty of people put in their ten thousand hours that makes for genius and never get the lucky break that brings overwhelming material success. This is a very likely scenario for most of us if we live on this planet.

There are, we can guarantee, other writers who may be as good as J. K. Rowling, other entrepreneurs who are easily as innovative and persistent as Elon Musk—and we will never know that they exist. These people did not get the lucky break, meet the right person at the right time, and get offered the opportunity that would catapult them into the international spotlight and make them rich and famous. Or maybe they did and then they were obscured by others—maybe their ideas were stolen, maybe their contributions changed the world but they got nothing for it. This is the reality of the world we have to live in.

It is logistically impossible for seven billion people to rise to the top of a pile. We are fed a constant diet of the myth of success and failure. We have been asked to believe that:

▶ People are successful when they have money, fame, and power.
▶ We all want and deserve this kind of success.
▶ Our hard work and dedication will pay off in the end if we truly put our minds to it.
▶ Material success is the ultimate goal of humanity.

Life tells us, though, that this isn't true.

Life has shown us that we operate outside the failure-success paradigm. We crave meaning and purpose that is beyond income and power and fame. We value our health, without which we cannot live. We value people and relationships.

But we live on a steady diet of failure and success stories. These are the particular myths that we buy into: that we should all have more and more and better and better stuff or fame or power and that hard work and putting our minds to it will reward us this way. Sometimes it might, but often it might not.

And that's perhaps where it's worth saying that the idea of failure itself is an invention, a story. We can explode the myth. We can write a new story.

Consider the fact that placing ourselves on the success-failure continuum may be creating billions of discontented people. Now let's look at people who could have been famous—but weren't.

## BOTOX

Since 2002, Botox has become the most famous injectable cosmetic, used on more than six million people a year in the United States to eliminate or soften wrinkles and frown lines. We all know the name and what people use it for. But before it found its way to fame as a wrinkle eliminator, the botulinum toxin was used therapeutically for all kinds of muscle spasms—despite the fact that in large doses, the toxin can cause paralysis of muscles due to interrupting the nerve signal. Canadian physician couple Jean and Alastair Carruthers used the toxin to help patients who suffered from disorders in which their eyes did not align properly. During treatments, they noticed the disappearance of wrinkles on the upper half of patient's faces—their frown lines miraculously vanished. Now this team began to help patients in a whole new way. What they didn't do was patent the drug for cosmetic purposes. Jean says, "I missed out on a fortune, but we have had the most enriching experience using it on patients over the years."[10]

Jean and Alastair may have missed out on their potential fortune, but their rewards came from elsewhere: they helped patients feel better about themselves. Their lives and work had meaning. Seen through the lens of the success/failure story, they failed to tap into the potential that should have been theirs. Someone else now rakes in the profits. Mention Botox at a dinner party, and everyone knows what you're talking about; start a conversation about Jean Carruthers, and we guarantee a round of silence or blank stares. The Carruthers are okay with that. They subscribe to another story about so-called failure and success.

There exist famous people and successful people as well as elements of modern life and culture that we take for granted and do not question. But every product and thing has a story behind it—people, dreams, trials and errors. And sometimes, despite the brilliance of an idea and the fact that it is as familiar to us as breathing, the inventors have vanished from our memories. Perhaps they made no money, received no fame. Are they still failures? Or have they given us something brilliant that enriches our lives?

## SIEGEL AND SHUSTER'S SUPERMAN

The success of the Superman icon is well known. Who has not heard of the Man of Steel in his many incarnations from the '30s though 2017? Whoever invented him must be one of the big success stories of the past ninety years, right? Yet the creators of Superman, Jerry Siegel and Joe Shuster, died in debt and spent most of their lives ensnared in legal battles to try to keep the Superman brand as their own. Their endeavours were successful in that Superman is a household name well into the twenty-first century, but they personally failed to reap the benefits of their invention.

From the very beginning, their efforts were dogged by failure. Siegel and Shuster created "The Superman" in 1933 and published a short story, "The Reign of the Superman," in Siegel's own fanzine, *Science Fiction #3*. Superman was not received well, so they modified him to become the character we know today and spent six years looking for a publisher who would be interested in him. The first bite Siegel and Shuster received was from Consolidated Book Publishing, but this company folded before they had a contract. Nevertheless, they persisted. In 1938, National Allied Publications (later to be DC Comics) featured "The Superman" on its cover of *Action Comics #1*.

How were they to know that "The Superman" would be a wildly successful multibillion-dollar industry for the next ninety years and counting? Siegel and Shuster sold the rights to National Allied Publications for $130 (equivalent to just over $2,000 today) and received a ten-year contract to write the stories for Action Comics. Selling themselves short was an act they could not undo for the rest of their lives.

Ten years later, in 1946, the pair sued the publisher to regain their rights to Superman, feeling that they had been robbed of their creation, but they lost their case. The New York State Supreme Court ruled that all rights had been "transferred to Detective Comics, Inc. . . . including the title, names, characters and conception . . ." and Shuster and Siegel's byline was subsequently removed from all Superman stories.[11]

When the Superman copyright came up again in 1967, Siegel unsuccessfully tried to sue for the rights to his creation and, though he had been writing for DC until then, was let go. In 1975, the pair publicly protested DC Comics's treatment of them and were each awarded a $20,000 (later $30,000) yearly stipend for the rest of their lives and the commitment that all Superman merchandise would credit them as Superman's creators. But they still felt that they didn't really get the massive money and credit they deserved.

Siegel worked for the rival company Marvel Comics for a while, for Archie Comics, for Charlton Comics, for the British comic *Lion*, and for Italy's Mondadori Editore, but when invited in 1986 by DC to write an "imaginary" Superman story, he declined. He died in 1996, excluded from the glories of the wild success his comic character had become.

Meanwhile, Shuster's worsening eyesight meant that he could no longer draw for a living, and he became a delivery man, rumoured to have delivered packages to the DC building itself. Shuster died a poor, indebted man in 1992. After his death, DC Comics paid his unpaid debts with the agreement that his estate would not challenge their ownership over Superman again. Yet in 1999, his widow and daughter filed a copyright termination notice and began another legal battle over the rights of the superhero, this time with Time Warner. And in 2006, yet another (unsuccessful) legal challenge was made, this time over their Superboy creation.

Siegel and Shuster's story is one of failure, and many

Superman fans believe these men were victims of a series of ruthless corporations who robbed them of their creative rights. Others argue that this was a failure of their own making. They did not foresee the potential of their invention and sold themselves short. Yet the creation itself must be considered the best success story of the comic industry. For over three generations, Superman has spawned comics, movies, TV series, and merchandise. Here are two men who failed—tragically, yes, but also brilliantly. Their legacy lives on. People are comforted, inspired, transported by their creative efforts long after the creators themselves lost everything and vanished. It is worth thinking about the nature of the Superman failure and understanding that there are perhaps millions of creative people and endeavours that are hijacked or obliterated. Despite the devastating outcome, we can't say that Superman is less valuable or that the work of these men came to nothing. They did not achieve the recognition they felt they deserved, but their creative efforts have changed our world.

Encouraging to note is the reason Jerry Siegel created Superman. It was not for fame or fortune or self-aggrandisement but altruism and empathy.

> What led me into creating Superman in the early thirties? . . . Hearing and reading of the oppression and slaughter of helpless, oppressed Jews in Nazi Germany . . . seeing movies depicting the horrors of privation suffered by the downtrodden. . . . I had the great urge to help . . . help the downtrodden masses, somehow. How could I help them when I could barely help myself? Superman was the answer.[12]

To bust the myth of failure fed to us by famous people, we have to bust the myth of success. Jerry Siegel's not-so-well-known motivation for Superman was a creative response to the horrors of the early twentieth century and the Holocaust.

The world needs us to be more than just economic units taking cues from a handful of gurus who presume to have the right to tell the rest of the human race that there is some magical formula for success and that they seem to have found it. There are many famous people who failed brilliantly before they succeeded; the only reason we know about them is because of their successes. There are also many invisible people who did not become famous and who nonetheless had a huge impact on our world. These people, too, failed brilliantly.

There is the chance, though, that these stories can be seen outside of the myths of success and failure. They are human stories of trial and error, and we do our society an injustice by marking them successes and failures—and by giving airtime only to those whose lives take them to the top of the pile. Most of us would have so much more in common with Siegel and Shuster than with J. K. Rowling or Elon Musk.

## BIG IDEAS

- ▶ When famous people lecture the masses on failure, they do so from a platform of extraordinary success and privilege.
- ▶ Plenty of people have brilliant ideas and inventions that do not get seen or rewarded, even though they have done every bit as much work as their well-known counterparts.
- ▶ We can't all be at the top of the material pile—it's logistically impossible.
- ▶ There is unquantifiable value to doing things for others, such as inspiring and comforting children with a comic or helping people feel better about themselves. It's worth remembering that these acts of generosity

give us emotional satisfaction regardless of whether they lead to financial rewards.

## HELPFUL THOUGHTS FOR BUSTING THE MYTHS OF FAILURE AND SUCCESS

▶ Allow yourself to be encouraged by stories of success, but explore deeper motivations for existing and working in the world.

▶ Don't beat yourself up when, despite your best efforts, you do not find yourself with an enormous bank account and worldwide fame. Learning to live without this is empowering.

▶ Imagine a dinner date with the Superman creators and what you might tell them about the value of their work in the world.

## NOTES

1. Zusak, Marcus. "The Failurist: Markus Zusak." TED Talk, Sydney, April 26, 2014. Accessed February 26, 2017. https://tedxsydney. com/talk/the-failurist-markus-zusak/.

2. Rowling, J. K. "Text of J. K. Rowling's Speech: The Fringe Benefits of Failure, and the Importance of Imagination." *Harvard Gazette*, June 5, 2008. Accessed August 22, 2016. http://news.harvard.edu/ gazette/story/2008/06/text-of-j-k-rowling-speech/.

3. Branson, Richard. "Turning failure into success." Virgin, January 5, 2017. Accessed August 22, 2016. https://www.virgin.com/ richard-branson/turning-failure-into-success.

4. Shah, Vishrut. "Elon Musk and the art of failing successfully." YourStory.com, June 28, 2016. Accessed August 22, 2016. https:// yourstory.com/2016/06/elon-musk-failure/.

5. D'Onfro, Jillian. "16 Genius Quotes from Eccentric Billionaire Elon Musk." *Business Insider Australia*, November 5, 2013. Accessed February 26, 2017. http://www.businessinsider.com.au/best-elon-musk-quotes-tesla-2013-11?r=US&IR=T#on-

government-licensing-we-have-essentially-no-patents-in-spacex-
our-primary-long-term-competition-is-in-china-if-we-published-
patents-it-would-be-farcical-because-the-chinese-would-just-use-
them-as-a-recipe-book-8.

6. Gladwell, *Outliers*.

7. "'Forbes' Billionaire List: JK Rowling Drops from Billionaire to
Millionaire Due to Charitable Giving." *Huffington Post*, March 15,
2012. http://www.huffingtonpost.com/2016/12/13/forbes-
billionaire-list-rowling_n_1347176.html.

8. Perhaps still mindful of her humble beginnings, J. K. Rowling has
gifted so much of her money away through her charitable orga-
nization and work with women in need that she has fallen off the
Forbes billionaire list, lost her billionaire status, and means to
keep on giving to those in poverty.

9. Furr, Nathan. "How Failure Taught Edison to Repeatedly
Innovate." *Forbes*, June 9, 2011. Accessed February 26,
2017. https://www.forbes.com/sites/nathanfurr/2011/06/09/
how-failure-taught-edison-to-repeatedly-innovate/#598cab4d65e9.

10. "The History behind the World's Most Popular Line and Wrinkle
Injectable." The Harley Medical Group, September 24, 2013.
Accessed March 14, 2017. https://www.harleymedical.co.uk/news/
the-history-behind-the-worlds-most-popular-line-and-wrinkle-
injectable#sthash.vywiLFho.dpufof.

11. Dean, Michael. "An Extraordinarily Marketable Man: The
Ongoing Struggle for Ownership of Superman and Superboy." *The
Comics Journal*, October 14, 2004. 263. Archived from the original
on September 19, 2008.

12. Andrae, Thomas, and Mel Gordon. *Siegel and Shuster's
Funnyman: The First Jewish Superhero, from the Creators of
Superman*. Port Townsend, WA: Feral House, 2010.

# CHAPTER SIX

# MOST PEOPLE ARE FAILURES

T he myth of failure and success we explored in Chapter Five is based on the dubious idea that we are all destined for material greatness and that those who don't make it have not worked hard enough, not paid their dues, or not done something-or-other that people who "make it" have done.

We construct a narrative in which our lives are supposed to go a certain way and when they don't, that constitutes a failure on our part. Hopefully we, the authors, have given enough good reasons to question that assumption. We know now that we can't always wholeheartedly believe what famous and successful people tell us about success and that we don't have to subscribe to the myth that the material success/failure continuum is the yardstick of our existence.

For most human beings, life is decidedly unfair. According to Oxfam's Credit Suisse Global Wealth Report, the wealth of the richest 1 percent of the world's population is equal to the wealth of the remaining 99 percent, including some of the most poverty-stricken regions on Earth.[1] That means that the cards, in various formats and in different scenarios, are pretty much stacked against ordinary people. In terms of financial success, the myth that if you try hard enough, you will achieve financial success beyond your wildest dreams is just that—a myth. A combination of tenacity and lucky breaks beyond our control leads to a few of us making it to the top of an inequitable pile. Being born in a village in Malawi or Burundi in Africa—the poorest countries on earth—would put you at a distinct disadvantage if you want to climb the proverbial ladder to material wealth. Worldwide, we buy the particular myth that somehow we all have the opportunity to make it if we just get it right. But we don't have equal opportunities. And, sure, some will still haul themselves out of circumstantial despair and begin to climb those ladders, but most won't. It's a gamble. The odds are against most of the world's population, and most of us will not achieve material success beyond our wildest dreams. We will fail many times over, and those failures will often not be the precursors to success. In this story, it doesn't matter how many times we turn failure into the good guy and sell failure as the courageous entrepreneur's voyage to blinding success, nor does it matter how many thousands of books on "failing better" crowd the bookstores—we are buying a fiction, the selling of an elite dream to masses of people who will continuously throw themselves into the race to be someone, get something, achieve greatness. The effects of cumulative third-degree failures can be seen in schools, universities, places of work, and homes.

So what do we do about that?

For many of us, when things go well, we think *Thank God* or even *There is a God!* When they don't go well, it is our fault—*we* haven't tried hard enough. This view compounds the sense that we are unworthy and undeserving and that our bad luck is some kind of punishment for doing things wrong. It's this view that we have the power to change, even as we accept that sad and bad things will happen to kind and good people.

# REAL-LIFE FAILURE STORIES

We are driven to chase success because it represents, at the most primal level, survival.

Let's give some space to the stories and perceptions of a few of the billions on the planet who have not at this moment achieved wealth, or fame, or power. They may, however, be able to give us insights that could turn out to be wiser and more helpful to us than the ones we get from those many famous and successful people.

Nicole Foreman[2] is a doctoral student in psychology who was living in San Diego until a year ago. At the end of her program, she had to apply for and complete a clinical internship and residency. All students were advised to apply to at least fifteen programs to ensure being invited to several interviews. She wrote:

> At the time, I was living in San Diego. I had a beautiful home literally on the beach. I would watch the sun set over the ocean nearly every day for about seven years. My family lived nearby. My boyfriend's family lived nearby. His family members even lived with us there for some time, and they would visit often. Friends would also visit often. So I applied for these internship programs, but only nine of them. I struggled to find programs to apply for because, ultimately, I wanted to stay in San Diego. There was one program in San Diego, and that was the only one I was interested in. When the invitations for interviews came out, I received an invite from every program except San Diego! I immediately realized that I would not be able to continue

living in San Diego if I moved forward with completing my doctoral degree. I felt embarrassed when I would face others with the news, especially when facing the people who previously tried to provide me with some assurance by saying things like "Of course you'll be invited to interview with San Diego! Of course you'll match there!" I felt I disappointed others as well, particularly family who wanted me to stay. I felt sorry for my boyfriend, who had followed me to San Diego from Santa Cruz to be with me, and wondered if he would decide to do the same when the time came to leave San Diego. So I would go for long runs along the ocean during sunset. I would often cry while running and take pictures of the sunset. Eventually I suppose the shock wore off and I had accepted that I would be moving. I didn't like that fact but didn't try battling it either. I decided that since I was no longer tied to San Diego, I could move forward with whatever was most appealing and desirable in that very moment. I interviewed with these other programs and paid very special attention to everything about them, from the program characteristics to the people, the culture, the setting, the geography, to how I felt while interviewing there and visiting the town, etc. Ultimately, I wound up matching at Brown University in Providence. It was my first choice after having reframed my attitude.

It's okay to feel nervous, sad, embarrassed. There's so much shame tied to these feelings, which I think amplifies them even more. And other people seem scared of, or uncomfortable with, these feelings—I never shared my experience with others, perhaps because I imagined they wouldn't know how to respond and I'd feel invalidated. Perhaps there is some value, though, in sharing these feelings with

others. Maybe sharing these feelings with others—
sharing feelings of sadness, nervousness, or embar-
rassment—can help reduce the stigma and shame
that's often tied to them. And maybe by sharing these
feelings, others will become more comfortable with
dealing with it, and responding, in a validating manner. Regardless, in this situation, I'm glad I accepted
the fact that I would be moving and glad I attempted
to make the most of it. I suppose an alternative
response could have been to stubbornly stay in San
Diego without completing my doctoral degree or to
select a mediocre program that was as close to San
Diego as possible. This reframe in thinking, and willingness to move forward despite the discomfort doing
so, provided me with some freedom that I didn't have
beforehand. It was quite liberating!

Nicole failed at first to get what she desperately wanted,
despite being an excellent student. At first, she could not see
how she could bear to leave San Diego. Once she realised that
an internship in her hometown was not going to materialise,
she was suddenly able to focus on everything else about her next
step that mattered to her. And that's the gift: the wisdom of ordinary failures and unexpected outcomes. There was a brilliant
opportunity for growth embedded in this unwanted outcome.
She had to contend with not only her own disappointment but
the responses of others, which she feared would invalidate her.
Yet she reframed her perspective and liberated herself.

We can't eliminate our deep-seated evolutionary drive to
get somewhere, to "make it." While taking lessons from famous
people on failure may motivate us, it does not protect us from
the reality that most of us must live with. We are not all going to
make a billion dollars or get what we want. We are not going to
be protected from illness, loss, and unwanted outcomes. But the
value in a so-called failure may be that we let go of a narrow idea

with a fixed outcome, as in Nicole's case, and embrace something unexpected that has significant value.

If we reevaluate the clichéd idea of "being a failure" in today's world through a changing lens, we might come up with some surprising insights.

Bertha spent her childhood in an orphanage in Ohio in the 1920s. Her father, Jacob, a poor refugee from Lithuania, spoke little English. He had begun his life with dreams of being a concert violinist, but persecution forced him to flee his homeland and go to America. As a new arrival with no English, he'd struggled to make a living for himself. Eventually he found work as a peddler, going from place to place selling odds and ends. He married the beautiful Ethel, and they had two children, Bertha and Meyer. But when the children were ages ten and seven, Ethel died of pneumonia. Of course, we could more accurately say that she died of poverty, as they were unable to afford the proper care to treat her curable condition. When his wife died and he found himself alone in the world with two young children, Jacob had no choice. He could not work as a fruit peddler and be a father to his children, so he sent them to the orphanage.

His dreams of making a new life in a new country did not come true. He spent the rest of his life scraping by, never having more than a rented room in someone's apartment and losing all his savings to the state department when he died. The children grew up, parented by the orphanage, and when Bertha turned twenty-two, a man in South Africa who had seen her photograph decided he wanted to marry her. He sent a marriage proposal, and she, with nothing to lose, accepted after his third letter. She left New York on the SS *Berengaria* in February 1938 and sailed first to London and then to South Africa. She was at sea for more than a month, and her heart was full of hope. She escaped the Great Depression and the freezing cold of the Midwest and thought she would be making a new life for herself in sunny South Africa. She had hopes that she would live a wonderful life, that she would be safe, comfortable, cared for.

But trouble loomed for her there as well: already a mass of dispossessed and disenfranchised black South Africans were stirring. By the time Bertha had married, settled down, and had a child, South Africa was beginning to show signs of unrest.

Bertha's sons grew up in the system of racial segregation in South Africa called apartheid. Civil society was affected on a daily basis by violence and unrest as the white minority government of the time held a black majority population in their control. Bertha lived through this unrest. On one occasion, she was attacked and left for dead when thieves beat her unconscious. They stole fifty cents from her wallet. Her son Bob tried to emigrate and take her with him, but that plan collapsed. Eventually all her grandchildren fled the violence of everyday South African life. She lived with her youngest son and his family until they were affected by crime and fled to Israel. She ended up penniless, living with her eldest son Bob and then later in an aged care facility at the end of her life, having lost her past, all her close friends in America, her history, and everything that had been familiar to her in her youth. Her hopes and dreams of a big, safe, successful life did not pan out. Her grandchildren had all left to go overseas. Bertha's life, in many ways, was like her father's life. It did not unfold as she dreamt it would when she was young. She died in her eighties. Her life had been a series of challenges and collapsed dreams.

And yet . . .

Would we call the lives of Jacob and his daughter failures?

If we measure our lives by material gains, then, indeed, they failed to achieve anything of note.

There were great losses, both financial and personal, for these generations. Jacob made no money, his daughter Bertha made no money, and later, Bertha's son Bob made no money, though all were smart, loving, and kind people. Jacob, Bertha, and Bob have left no noticeable trace in the world. They left nothing but the faintest echo of their lives in Bertha's letters and diaries, discovered in a box in 2012 by her granddaughter, Shelley—the coauthor of this book.

In 2016, exactly one hundred years after Bertha was born, the biographical memoir of Bertha and Jacob's lives *Whisperings in the Blood* was published by the University of Queensland Press in Australia.[3] Shelley wrote the book to honour the lives of her refugee ancestors and to connect herself and her readers with the lives of immigrants everywhere. The journeys and lives of this family were now being shared across the world.

Bertha had kept all her letters and diaries from 1938 onward, and in 2014, when Shelley began to write about the struggles of her ancestors, she realised that her own life was an echo of Bertha's. Writing the book became not only a generational healing but a personal healing, for finally, after five continents and a hundred years of searching for home, Jacob, Bertha, and Bob's descendants found that home in Australia. The book has since received excellent reviews and a flood of fan mail; readers have been moved and changed by the lives and the struggles of Jacob and Bertha and Bob. A producer is interested in turning the book into a TV series.

"This book changed me," one reader wrote. "It is beautiful. I am in love with Bertha. Reading about her makes me treasure my own grandmother so much."[4]

Far from slipping into invisibility, Jacob and Bertha and Bob now live on as characters whose courage and love are an inspiration to readers in the present day—an unexpected miracle. The immigrant lives of Bertha and her family allow readers to feel empathy for the immigrant experience. More than a century after Jacob made his journey across the sea, he and his descendants are loved by unknown strangers in a future he could not have imagined. There was and continues to be meaning in these lives that have been full of all kinds of struggle—and the meaning has nothing to do with financial success.

The way we measure things and quantify our lives leaves much to be desired. The emphasis we place on what is important creates the expectations and rules by which we live. We fail to imagine the deeper threads of meaning that run through our lives and connect us to the things that really matter.

We have embraced a material set of criteria, and we measure and are constantly measured by these criteria—even though so many of us know that this is not all there is to life. We know it, but we don't believe it, and few of us live by it.

In terms of everything we assume about failure—that it has to do with the acquisition of wealth and material success as described by many famous and wealthy people—Jacob, Bertha, and Bob would be termed "failures."

Yet their lives have brought insight and compassion and given joy and pleasure to thousands of readers in the twenty-first century. We have to learn to look at our life narratives from a much wider, wiser vantage point.

# MONEY DOES NOT EQUAL HAPPINESS

We need a certain amount of money to survive, to feed and clothe and educate ourselves and our families, and to take care of medical emergencies when they arrive. There's no doubt about it—having money makes things easier. Below a certain amount (which varies from country to country because of the buying power of the currency), life is an uphill struggle for survival. For the United States, we even have a figure, a magic number that marks a watershed: in 2010, Daniel Kahneman and Angus Deaton analysed about 450,000 responses to the Gallup-Healthways Well-Being Index. A thousand Americans were asked on a daily basis about their emotional well-being and about their life evaluation.

Kahneman and Deaton found a number: up to $75,000 per annum as an income, having more money made life easier and made people happier. But after that? "Beyond $75,000 in the contemporary United States, however, higher income is neither the road to experienced happiness nor the road to the relief of unhappiness or stress."[5]

It seems that once we have achieved that $75K, our experience of the world is largely dependent on our attitude. Below that amount, we suffer from low life-evaluation and more emotional pain when things go wrong, when partners leave, when health issues arise. Above that amount, we have a higher life-evaluation in that we *think* our lives have more value and are better, but we are no happier—nor do we feel less stressed. In other words, we can't buy happiness beyond a certain point (that point being $75,000).

With that established, let's say we keep the old idea of personal failure in mind. We might draw a line and say, "Well, if you're earning over $75K, you're all good. You've made it. You are a success. Quit complaining and change your attitude."

But then three realities have to be considered:

1. At the time of Kahneman and Deaton's research, the mean US household income was $71,500. Only a third of households showed incomes above $75,000. This means that two-thirds of earners in the United States got below Kahneman and Deaton's magical $75K ideal of 2010.

2. We are all affected by the fact that we quickly become accustomed to what we have. Even if we get a raise or a promotion, the feel-good effect is temporary before that new number becomes "normal."

3. If two-thirds of Americans fail to meet the basic income amount for a feeling of emotional well-being, then two-thirds of Americans—most people—are feeling like failures. They have low life-evaluation.

So we are going to be similarly happy with $75K or $85K, and we're not going to be able to sustain the feel-good effect of a

promotion or a raise anyway, because pretty soon we'll be looking for the next rung on the ladder. And even though two-thirds
of Americans may have low life-evaluation, we might keep this
in mind: Kahneman and Deaton suggest in their research that
those people who earn more money seem to have a "reduced
ability to savor small pleasures."[6] So once you're super rich,
it's going to be arguably harder to get pleasure out of the small
and subtle things in life that you enjoy when you're making an
adequate living! In other words, there is something we can do
regardless of how much we earn. We can build a sense of self, a
sense of purpose that is not tied to our earning capacity or lack
thereof. This approach won't solve all our problems, but it will
go some way towards making life easier. Once we've earned our
$75K which gives us everything we need, our feeling of being
"rich," the way we evaluate our lives, is subjective and highly
contextual. If everyone lives in a hut on the edge of the sea, then
we feel as well off as the guy next door. If our neighbours have
opulent houses with massive pools, then we don't value a small
brick home highly. We feel poor regardless of how much we
actually have.

If we take a critical look at ourselves and the accepted norms
and behaviours of the society we live in, we have the power to
effect change that may have an impact our happiness and even
how long we live.

Our measurement of a successful or a failed life is, unfortunately for us, dictated by a media frenzy that suggests 24/7 that
more and more is better and better, that failing to get more is
failing intrinsically, and that we are what we earn. We measure
our lives mostly by the ratio of feelings of happiness and success
to unhappiness and distress, yet our lives are often made up of a
series of wrong turns and brick walls, of innovating against the
odds, of finding ways that work when others don't. We might do
well to see these merely as things that will happen: these are the
forces that play a role in shaping us. The word *failure*, however,
does a disservice to our endeavours when we let it define us.

Here's a thought that has its root in ancient practices. What if we measured our lives by the immeasurable? By how much we love and are loved in return, by the distance we travel to overcome daily hurdles, to survive, by the way we treasure being alive, by the qualities we exhibit, the millions of unrecorded and unnoticed transactions that take place every second of every day that affect our lives and the lives of those around us?

There are billions of people who survive living hard lives, like Jacob and his family. But these people lived and do live a life of purpose. They love. They are loved in return. Each day, for generations, these people have made discoveries about others, about life and living; they live through tragedies and laughter. These people are us, and we are them.

We live lives that have limitless potential that is not measurable, and when we impose measurement on it, we are vulnerable to the disease of dissatisfaction, greed, stress, "keeping up with the Joneses," and a disposition that makes us susceptible to the very tangible effects of stress and unhappiness.

# NEAR-DEATH EXPERIENCES

We do not have to be financially rich or be famous or have lots of stuff to be fulfilled. Just ask anyone who has had a near-death experience whether the same things that mattered before the event still matter afterwards—or whether their relationship to material gain has changed.

Money makes life easier—absolutely. Material possessions help us in many ways. But we can rest assured that money is not likely to make us happier beyond a certain point. The guy who dies with the most toys at the end is not the winner.

If life is a process and that life has purpose, then we cannot judge ourselves and others by the media-induced criteria of success and failure. Any fabulously materially privileged person who says "I was a big failure, and now I'm a big success" just casts a depressing grid over the rest of the population and makes them feel inadequate, poor, less than someone else. Though famous people rave about the value of failure in order to motivate or to sell things, the concept that you have to get lots of stuff to be a success devalues our human struggles, our striving, our heroic strengths in surviving and dealing with adversity.

From what we know now, we might argue that a life fully lived is not a failure. Yes, it may be full of heartbreak and unanticipated and unwanted outcomes, but at the end, at the very end, all our lives . . . end. We fail to get up one morning, and the world continues without us. We don't go to funerals as if they are some kind of grand finale, a moment when we tally someone's achievements and pronounce them a success or a failure. We go to honour the person and who they were and to show the ones left behind that the person mattered, that all of their achievements, struggles, personal qualities, and kindnesses are valued. That we cared and do care.

And if we don't measure our lives at the *very end* by how much stuff we have accumulated or how many achievements we can count, then why should we *ever*?

It's time to stop measuring our lives in this way, because the measurement tool is faulty.

One of the most interesting perspectives on life and its value comes from people who have had near-death experiences (NDEs). Whether these people escape death by a narrow margin or have transcendent spiritual experiences, research shows that the experience has a profound and long-lasting effect on people's lives, how they live them, and their life-evaluation.

Invariably, people confronted with dying or near death seem to completely shift their perspective of what's important and what has meaning. This shift can be a gift for those of us who too easily get caught up on the stress freeway, chasing after material dreams and success, desperate not to fail. These people provide us with profound insights. We don't have to have faced death ourselves to understand and value the wisdom they share.

Ric Elias is an executive who heads the marketing company Red Ventures. He is also a survivor of Flight 1549, which crash-landed in the Hudson River in January 2009, guided to safety by the skill and aptitude of Captain Chesley Sullenberger ("Sully").

Elias says he learned a few things as a *bang* shook the engine and the plane turned. He reevaluated his whole life in a very short time—the time when he thought his death was imminent. His only prayer was that the plane would blow up. He didn't want it to break apart; he wanted to die instantly. And he said he realised in those moments that there was sadness in dying—but no fear. Dying, he said, is not scary. But the sadness that came was regret tied to those he loved and would leave behind.

> I thought about, wow, I really feel one real regret. I've lived a good life. In my own humanity and mistakes, I've tried to get better at everything I tried. But in my humanity, I also allow my ego to get in. And I regretted the time I wasted on things that did not matter with people that matter. And I thought about my relationship with my wife, with my friends, with people. And after, as I reflected on that, I decided to eliminate negative energy from my life. It's not perfect, but it's a lot better. I've not had a fight with my wife in two years. It feels great. I no longer try to be right; I choose to be happy.[7]

In the years since the crash, his purpose for living has changed completely. Above all, he values being a father. The only mission of this high-flying executive is to be a great dad.

Success and failure have little to do with anything material and everything to do with being the most loving, giving human being to the people who matter most in his life.

I was given the gift of a miracle, of not dying that day. I was given another gift, which was to be able to see into the future and come back and live differently. I challenge you guys that are flying today, imagine the same thing happens on your plane—and please don't—but imagine, and how would you change? What would you get done that you're waiting to get done because you think you'll be here forever? How would you change your relationships and the negative energy in them?[8]

These insights allow us a rare glimpse into the things that really matter. We don't have to be in a plane crash. We can wake up tomorrow and dissolve the all the stresses and angst of "trying to make it."

One of the most awe-inspiring stories is that of Anita Moorjani's near-death experience. Her story, as told in her book *Dying to Be Me*, has become one of the most well-documented and publicized NDEs. The experience itself is one thing, and regardless of what we believe in, the aftereffects have changed Anita's life and may have inspirational value for all of us and how we choose to live our lives.

The biggest lesson I learned was how important it was to love myself and be true to myself. That is the most important lesson from my NDE. I had always thought it was selfish to love myself and meet my needs before others, but I learned that if I do not love myself, I will not have enough love to give others, because I cannot give others what I myself do not have. The more I love myself and have my own needs met, the easier it is for me to be generous with others.[9]

In 2002, Anita Moorjani was living in Singapore when she was diagnosed with lymphoma. All her life, she had feared cancer and had done all she could to prevent it, so the diagnosis was a terrible blow. By 2006, despite trying every natural and chemical remedy under the sun, she had reached the end stages of her disease and was admitted to the hospital as her organs began to shut down. She lost consciousness, and her family was called in. It was then, she said, that she felt herself "transition into the other realm." In a 2015 video interview with *The Manifes-Station*, she says that before she lost consciousness, she was in "total pain. I would not wish this on my worst enemy. I couldn't lie down without choking. My skin opened up in lesions. . . . It was the most painful thing."[10]

While her body slipped into a thirty-five-hour coma, she went into a space where she says time was not linear. She was "met" by deceased friends and relatives, specifically her father and her best friend who had died of cancer. She said, "I learned what caused my cancer. I learned it wasn't my time and I had to come back. . . . In the clarity of the NDE, I understood this was just my own energy turned against me. It was a reflection of my own beliefs about myself."[11]

During her time in a coma, she heard and saw what was happening in the hospital room as well as down the corridor and further afield.

> I had so much clarity as to why I had the cancer, why I was in that situation. . . . I could see my life, every decision, every thought I had in my entire life. . . . I could see why I was there. If I summed it up in one word, that would be fear. I feared not being good enough, displeasing people . . . not meeting expectations . . . not being spiritual enough . . . death . . . the afterlife; I feared cancer, chemotherapy. I also feared things that I believed caused cancer—mobile phones, microwaves.[12]

During those moments when everyone around her thought she was dead, her out-of-body experience changed her life. She says she was given a message while she was there, and the message was that if she chose to come back, her cancer would heal within a short time.

When she came around and opened her eyes, her family was astonished. These were supposed to be her final hours. But they couldn't have been more stunned than her doctors. Though she was given chemotherapy for a few weeks, the rapid disappearance of every single trace of cancer was unprecedented. After five weeks, her massive tumours and lesions, her weeping sores, every possible trace of cancerous growth vanished. Oncologist Dr. Peter Ko from California flew out to meet the staff at the hospital in Hong Kong where Anita had been and looked at her medical records. He couldn't understand how she had made such a rapid and miraculous recovery. Later, other oncologists from around the world investigated her case and were likewise baffled that she was even alive. But perhaps what is most compelling is how her life changed after this experience. Like Ric Elias, Anita's focus in life shifted completely. She understood that she had now found her life's purpose. She advocates not treating anything in our lives as a battle.

> Work with it. Whether it's life, or cancer, or job loss, or any challenge. Embrace it. Love where you are now. Listen to what it's trying to tell you; identify what gifts it's brought you. Life and disease and struggle in every form is not a race or a battle. . . . Don't obsess over things . . . illness . . . job losses . . . we lose ourselves then. We obsess about the financial situation or the health situation and we make every day about battling. The cancer is the best gift I ever had. . . . That cancer saved my life. I wouldn't change that for anything. . . . I used to believe I had to pursue things. . . .

> My life was like a race. I used to work in the corporate
> field . . . it was very, very competitive. Now, I would
> never go back to that. I don't see time in the same way.
> I don't see that we're in a race against time. Everything
> exists simultaneously.[13]

We should find that which brings us joy. Most importantly, she asks us to "get out of that state of fear,"[14] reminding us to do the things in the world that make our hearts sing rather than what we feel obliged to do.

## CHANGING OUR PERSPECTIVE

We live lives that are full of fear of failure: we fear failing ourselves, our partners, our dreams, our children. We fear our health failing, losing our jobs, and our children failing at school, failing at life. We have entrepreneurs and writers and innovators and scientists telling us to embrace failure and to fail more and better. But in the end, the language of failure is creating us and our lives, and this makes us feel small and crushed. Most of us will live ordinary lives punctuated by extraordinary experiences. In material terms, most of us will be failures at one time or another.

So it might help us to slowly begin to erase the concept of our lives as a series of goal-setting and goal-getting activities. What if we just forget the idea of life as a race with a finish line and replace that idea with the idea of life as a journey? There are hurdles and challenges along the way. Some we overcome, some will set us back, but as long as we are alive on this journey, our lives have purpose.

We make that purpose.

If our purpose is to gather things and amass wealth and power, we may well succeed at that, but it won't make us any happier than the guy down the street earning his $75K. If our purpose is to live each day as fully as possible, then regardless of what we have or achieve, we may, according to the insights of Ric Elias and Anita Moorjani, live lives full of joy and meaning and purpose. If we're looking for inspiration, it makes sense to find it in the real stories of real people who live their lives outside the continuum of success and failure.

## BIG IDEAS

▶ The wealth of the richest 1 percent of the world's population is equal to the wealth of the remaining 99 percent. In terms of achieving huge success, the cards are stacked against most people.

▶ Letting go of a fixed goal in order to embrace something unexpected can be valuable. According to research, earning more than a certain amount ($75K in the United States) does not increase happiness.

▶ Our measurement tool for what really matters in life is faulty.

▶ Ordinary people who have almost died show us that the ideas of success and failure lose all meaning when you are confronted with the possibility of death.

## HELPFUL THOUGHTS FOR CHANGING HOW WE THINK ABOUT SUCCESS AND FAILURE

▶ Let go of some fixed goals, like "I have to make enough money to retire by the time I'm fifty." Or, "I have to get married by the time I'm thirty." Or, "I have to have so much in the bank before I can relax." There is so much that can happen to prevent your reaching these goals that is beyond your control.

▶ Stop worrying about the small stuff. If your plane is about to go down, what would you regret the most? Get up tomorrow and do something so that you will never have that regret.

▶ Remember that the feel-good effect of success is temporary. You will soon be compelled to start chasing the next dream. Enjoy the moment. The whole of life is made up of a string of moments. Right now is the only reality.

▶ Stop equating having more and better stuff with personal value. You are as unique and valuable as anyone, regardless of the amount you earn, how famous you are, or the car you drive.

## NOTES

1. Davidson, Jacob. "Yes, Oxfam, the Richest 1% Have Most of the Wealth. But That Means Less Than You Think." *Time*, January 21, 2015. Accessed March 14, 2017. http://time.com/money/3675142/oxfam-richest-1-wealth-flawed/.

2. Nicole Foreman. Interview with authors, 2017. Name changed for privacy.

3. Davidow, Shelley. *Whisperings in the Blood*. Brisbane, Australia: University of Queensland Press, 2016.

4. Personal correspondence. Shelley Davidow. February 2017.

5. Kahneman, Daniel, and Angus Deaton. "High income improves evaluation of life but not emotional well-being." *Proceedings of the National Academy of Sciences* 107, no. 38 (2010): 16489–93.

6. Ibid.

7. Elias, Ric. "3 things I learned while my plane crashed." Ted Talk, 2011. Accessed October 18, 2016. https://www.ted.com/talks/ric_elias/transcript?language=en.

8. Ibid.

9. Pastiloff, Jennifer. "Dying to Be Me. The Manifestation Q&A Series: Anita Moorjani." The Manifes-Station, February 6, 2012. Accessed March 3, 2017. http://themanifeststation.net/2012/02/06/dying-to-be-me-the-manifestation-qa-series-anita-moorjani/.

10. Ibid.

11. "21 Life Lessons from Anita Moorjani's Amazing Near Death Experience." *Conscious Life News*, January 22, 2015. Accessed October 18, 2016. http://consciouslifenews.com/ life-lessons-anita-moorjanis-death-experience-video/1135078/.

12. Ibid.

13. Ibid.

14. Ibid.

## SUGGESTED READING

Moorjani, Anita. *Dying to Be Me: My Journey from Cancer, to Near Death, to True Healing*. London: Hay House, 2014.

# CHAPTER SEVEN

# THE LANGUAGE OF FAILURE

n 2013, the second-most used word on the internet was "fail" after error code 404, which means the same thing:

> 404 is the near-universal numeric code for failure on the global Internet, augmenting its original use as "page not found." The single word *fail* is often used together with 404 to signify complete failure of an effort, project, or endeavor.[1]

The term *404* actually refers to a room number—it was in room 404 on the fourth floor that the first database, which was to become the World Wide Web, found its early home at CERN in Switzerland. Here, a group of enthusiastic young scientists and entrepreneurs created the error code way back in the dark ages of the 1990s.[2] The world has added another connotation to the word *failure*, which has steadily been shifting in meaning for centuries. If we're writing a whole book devoted to exploding the myth of failure, it makes sense to investigate the language of failure and the word itself, which have become a pervasive part of our lives.

# A BRIEF HISTORY OF *FAILURE*

Of the more than one million words in use in the English language and the almost 600 million people writing English content on the internet, *fail* and the concept of failure currently top the charts!

The word *fail* emerged in the 1200s from Old French *falir*, which meant "to be lacking," "to come to an end," "to be dying," or "let down" and from the Latin *fallere*, which meant "to trip" or "cause to fall" in a literal sense and "to trick, dupe, cheat, be defective" in the figurative. Before the 1200s, the Old English word had been *abreoðan*, which meant "to perish" or "to be destroyed." From about the early 1300s, the word *fail* meant "to run short of" and was used only to refer to goods, things, and foods. Beyond the mid-1300s, the word *fail* expanded to the failure of things and objects and meant "break down" or "go to pieces." After the 1300s, the word sometimes referred to human experiences as well and meant "to suffer loss of vigour," to "fail in courage," or to "fail in strength." It was in the late 1200s that the Anglo-French version of the word, *failer*, began to be used as the noun *failure*. Only in 1837 did the word come to be used as a broad term that defined a person, as in "he was a total failure."[3]

This is significant because we can see over time how the word *failure* has evolved and shifted in its meaning and observe how it has entered the twenty-first century and the significant role it plays in all our lives. Less than two hundred years ago, you could not be termed a "failure." Now we're almost glued to the concept of being a success or a failure.

As we know, every living species has been competing and winning and losing the battle to exist for the whole of evolution. This pattern of trial and error is the model that underpins everything. We are not fixed. We are in process all the time; we are evolutionary. Words are evolutionary too.

We use the word *fail* these days in so many contexts. Type the word *fails* into Google preceded by any noun, and you're rewarded with a series of hilarious disasters—"dog fails," "cat fails," "guy fails," "girl fails," "wedding fails." What makes for humour and laughter is that the outcome is unexpected. Neither the cat trying to catch the fish nor the person filming the cat knew that the cat would fall into the fish tank. The unexpected outcome is now an internet "fail" sensation.

There are a million ways in which things don't work every day. But the language we use and hear, which enables us to communicate what and how we think, also shapes our realities and our beliefs. If it didn't, writers wouldn't still be sitting in prisons all over the world, journalists wouldn't be facing prosecution, presidential debates would get no viewers, and newspapers would have no readers. No one would post rants on Facebook, and no one would rant back. Words matter. Words can change our minds. We base our votes, our buying, our education, and our beliefs on words and their power to move us. The pen—or the keyboard—is still as feared by regimes across the world as an armed invasion by aliens. Whistleblowers who leak documents are exiled and imprisoned, and people want to kill these guys for the words they put out. Governments the world over fear words and what they can do.

Evidently, words have immense power, and it matters how we use them. So if the words *failure* and *fail* are some of the most-used words in world, this must have an effect. We've all experienced how it shapes our beliefs and values. What does it mean for our lives that so much of what we do is termed "failure" and that we have attached so much stigma to that word in so many contexts?

By 1837, society began to market a concept of personal failure to the masses by using it in the context of someone actually being a failure. Does that mean that humans never considered themselves unworthy or lacking? No, of course not. But calling someone a "failure" is giving them a terminal label—a label that didn't exist before and that has now grown and seeped into our education systems, our medical systems, and our personal lives.

Of course, our emotions around not reaching our goals, not making enough money, not getting the jobs we want—all of that has been there for all of evolution in different ways and will continue to be a part of our lives. But the complex and imaginary structures we have imposed on our lives and the way we live them is created by us, by the language we use and believe in.

The words *fail* and *failure* are overused; we apply them to our lives in numerous contexts every day, and we're often oblivious to how our perceptions of ourselves and others are affected by the concept of failure.

## FEAR OF FAILURE

When we lock ourselves into this way of seeing the world as though it is the only one that exists, we create a reality that we now find hard to escape.

People are trying.

The group that claims "failure is good," "fail more; fail better" is really trying.

But they are up against the very definition and terminal nature of the idea of failure. Personal, financial, and academic failure has such a stigma attached to it and creates so much shame that people go to ridiculous lengths to avoid being seen as failures.

Without this stigma and fear, we wouldn't see the devastating results of failure. In *Black Box Thinking*, Matthew Syed proposes that the fear of shame and failure in medicine and in the criminal justice system in particular leads to people holding onto their version of reality even when irrefutable evidence shows otherwise, a state he coins "cognitive dissonance."[4]

It's true! When faced with evidence that cannot be refuted, otherwise intelligent people will still cling to their own ideas to save face. This includes, for example, high court judges who won't let an accused go even when DNA evidence and the actual perpetrator are irrefutably in existence. Syed tells stories of judges and juries evolving elaborate theories to support their assumptions of a person's guilt regardless of DNA and other evidence. Why? Shame. People do not like to be wrong because of how society views failure. If you failed to identify the criminal in the first place, that makes you look bad. So keep the guy you first caught because it shows you in a good light. Some people would risk lives and morals just to remain right. Our desire to avoid shame or blame or both is at the heart of every lie and cover-up under the sun. Syed refers to a medical case in which during an operation, a chief surgeon refused to remove his latex gloves even when his patient exhibited obvious signs of a latex allergy. The patient was in grave danger of dying, but the lead surgeon removed his gloves only under threat from his colleague that he would phone a superior immediately and reveal what was happening. This colleague luckily happened to be a researcher on medical errors. He had lost his own father to medical error and could see that they were in danger of losing this patient because of the cognitive dissonance of the surgeon overseeing the operation. Only after the colleague's threat did the surgeon remove his gloves. The patient survived.[5]

Cover-ups, lies, and avoiding shame and blame are all the by-products of a culture where failing in one way or another is regarded as the worst possible outcome. If a military exercise fails or a war looks like it is going to be lost, propaganda and story-spinners step in to create alternate scenarios that support whichever regime or ideology they are trying to uphold. Words are used in tricky and convoluted ways to prevent the word *failure* from coming to the fore.

If we are anxious about an exam, we would rather cheat to pass than risk failing. Deaths because of medical errors do not often make it out into the light. There are few places where grave errors and first-degree failures are acknowledged and protocols put in place to avoid subsequent errors. The airline industry is the best-known area where this does happen and, in *Black Box Thinking*, becomes the gold standard against which we might measure how we tackle failures in other areas.

We have created an aversion to failure by our responses to it in every facet of life. Before we move on to what we actually do to address this unhelpful state of affairs, let's look at one of the areas where the language of failure begins for many of us and where the root of so many problems relating to the concept of failure actually lies.

# FAILING AT SCHOOL AND BEYOND

All over the world, millions and millions of children sit exams. End-of-school exams are the most obvious example of how we have created a culture of fear around the word *failure*. The lengths people will go to avoid the shame and anxiety that go with failing final school exams is extreme. Across the world, particularly in India and other Asian countries, there have been spates of high-profile suicides amongst young people linked to the shame and fear of not succeeding in school. The language of failure is on every handout on every assignment throughout schools, affecting millions and millions of children every single day. *Did I fail? Did you get an A?* And sometimes the answer means life or death. Thousands of children commit suicide every year fearing an F or a low grade on a final exam paper.[6]

How can anyone resist the powerful impact of the language of failure at home and at school? Kids are being judged on an A–F scale from the minute they can understand the world. First and foremost, they learn to fear failure, or Fs. We can't try to say to them later on that really, failing is good and it teaches you something, because they know that failing is bad. It brings on ridicule and bullying from other kids, it brings derision from teachers and disappointment from parents who have some- how welded their children's school result to a primal survival instinct. In the United States, suicide is the second-leading cause of death in the ten- to twenty-four-year-old age group. School environments are at the core of many kids' feelings of lack of self-worth, depression, and helplessness. It's where this fear of failure starts for a lot of people.

> Youths may feel rising stress from the more competitive school environment. Rising income disparities put more onus of doing well in school: i.e., to be winners in the process rather than the losers. Depressed students cope less well as the pressures increase over time.[7]

In the first phase of a nationwide enquiry into suicides committed by 145 people under twenty-five in the United Kingdom, researchers at the University of Manchester identified "relevant antecedents" prior to suicide by young people. Between 2014 and 2015, almost a third of the young people still at school who committed suicide were either "facing exams or exam results at the time of death."[8]

How deeply unnerving that a young person, full of life and talent and potential, would rather die than face an exam or the results of an exam! But we need to remember that we have created these third-degree failures out of thin air. Teachers and legislators decide that a certain benchmark is a "pass" and another is a "fail." One is a stamp of approval, and another tells you you're worthless.

Something is wrong with our set of expectations and the way we use them. Our A–F grading system is a societal blight that does not mirror the actual world of human endeavour or evolution. School feeds children a set of expectations that we have created where a ladder of success leads some kids to be winners and some losers. Yet we know from looking at second-degree failures and every entrepreneurial, creative, or human endeavour that has led to an unexpected outcome that there is an entirely different approach that we can take to this winner/loser paradigm.

The real world does not operate on an A–F scale. The real world offers every one of us a series of unanticipated outcomes. We often don't get what we want or what we're aiming for, but other things happen along the way. As long as we are alive, we are going to be at pains to suggest that failure is a good thing. The word *failure* is a terminal concept; it does not allow us to evolve.

We need a radical approach to how we look at failure. We need to erase the word *failure* in schools and academic institutions; the concept of personal failure will eventually go with it. If we can erase failure from school dialogue, no child will ever be told that they have failed, that they are less worthy than someone else. Students will be motivated to learn, not to avoid failure.

The reason why getting an F on an exam is worse than dying for some is because the idea of personal failure has become inseparable from exam results. F means you are a failure. You are not smart enough. You are worse than everyone else, lower, not worthy.

These academic failures are third-degree failures. They are arbitrary results based on invented standards that vary from country to country, from state to state, that report on a narrow band of outcomes which suit a narrow band of children. We have created a culture around the idea of failure that defines us, and we should be able to un-create it, to dissolve it.

Our common discourse is one of failure and success, of shame and blame and fame, and this does not make our lives happier or better nor does it make us more effective at what we do.

# RENAMING FAILURE

We cannot turn the word *failure* into the good guy as long as it exists in the punitive model by which we educate our children and evaluate our lives. We fear failure. It's a survival thing. We have to replace it with another concept, one that is capable of providing us with the language of growth, of overcoming, of trying again.

The things we call failures are often nothing of the sort, and our language needs to evolve to reflect that.

The language we use influences the way we think, just as our language also reflects the way we think. Stanford University psychology professor Lera Boroditsky has shown in her research how fundamentally the language we use shapes our thoughts. She's even shown how people who speak different languages think about certain objects differently according to each object's grammatical gender.

> The grammar we learn from our parents, whether we realize it or not, affects our sensual experience of the world. Spaniards and Germans can see the same things, wear the same clothes, eat the same foods, and use the same machines. But deep down, they are having very different feelings about the world about them.[9]

For example, the noun "bridge" is feminine in German (*die Brücke*). In Spanish, the noun is masculine (*el puente*). When Boroditsky asked native German speakers to give a description of a bridge, they came up with words like "beautiful, elegant, slender." Native Spanish speakers, on the other hand, responded to the same question with words like "strong, sturdy, towering."[10]

In this way, we can see how the word *failure* in English is profoundly associated with a negative and inescapable outcome. Add to this the fact that our brains retain negative information far more easily than positive information, and the necessity of tackling failure at a linguistic level becomes obvious.

Our negative bias is evolutionary. We are here because we learned how to avoid, outwit, and outrun danger, so we've always held onto negative information for survival. Our brains evolved in a way that would ensure we would take note of what represented a threat or danger very early on in our lives so that we could stay clear of it. And things haven't changed at that level.

In his studies at Ohio State University, University of Chicago professor of psychology John Cacioppo showed how the participants' brains responded to scary and horrible images with much greater electrical activity in the cerebral cortex than when participants were shown positive or neutral images.[11] This means we need a far greater ratio of positive images to counter the effect of negative images. For every word and thought associated with failure, we need many more to reframe the experience and reflect it differently.

It's therefore a mammoth effort, we agree, to begin to shift the way we speak about and think about failure. But it's a worthy shift to make—and one we can accomplish.

## SHIFTING OUR PERCEPTION OF FAILURE

Synonyms for *failure* are always negative. *Failure* and its synonyms are infiltrating our language and the way we shape our world every hour of every day. If we call ourselves, our actions, and others by these words, it's a form of abuse, and our brains are going to hold onto those negative biases like crazy. But if we want to live more positively, we have to change the way we use our language. Because we're alive and because our lives are in movement all the time, we can't believe in these terminal verdicts as long-lasting assessments. Life is a process, and negative words combined with our very human tendency towards negative bias can confine us to the point where we can't see our way out.

Here's a story that exemplifies how we might start out and where we might go if we want to change the way we speak to ourselves and others about failure.

Peter Croft[12] is a man whose life has seemed to be made up of one disaster after another. He sees himself as a failure. He is fifty this year. He had goals in life, but he has not achieved them. He keeps saying to himself, *That last move was a disaster; that relationship was a waste of time; this is the third time we have made a bad decision about housing; I always end up giving in to my boss.*

This pattern of failure is reinforced more and more. What chance does he have of making any decisions that will allow him to feel better, more confident, more hopeful, if he now labels himself a failure and creates neural pathways that channel and reinforce his belief in himself as a failure? He's building the loser effect into his responses to the world, and the more he does it with his words and thoughts, the truer it is for him. He needs to change the language of failure in his life. How?

We are most often completely unaware of how language shapes us, how our self-talk and the way we load our stories and histories can influence who we are, shape our view of the world. Let's rewrite Peter's story and choose antonyms that are still true but which throw a positive light on Peter's story and don't paint the picture of him as a failure.

Peter Croft is a man whose life has been full of challenges. He sees himself as an explorer. He is fifty this year. He had goals in life, and he feels hopeful that his journey will still reveal some pleasant surprises. He keeps saying to himself, *That last move was essential; that relationship taught me a lot about myself; this is the third time I have been challenged by the house I've bought; I've finally realized that I do have the presence of mind to stand up to my boss.*

The story is the same, but the slant is different. There is no hint in the language that Peter is a loser. He's the same guy; we're just replacing the language of failure with the language of human endeavour. If Peter told himself and others the second story every day, his experience of the world would perhaps shift.

We all need to do this in our daily lives. We need to change the way we think about ourselves and others, focus on the positive rather than the negative, and be aware that by using the language of failure, we are reinforcing the habit of a negative worldview on ourselves and others that is difficult to break. By changing our language, we can change our thoughts and our actions.

## BIG IDEAS

► The word *fail* is the second–most used word on the internet in English.

► Kids across the world commit suicide either before, during, or after exams because they fear being seen as failures if they don't get the marks they or their parents or teachers expect of them.

► Our common discourse is one of failure and success, of shame and blame and fame. This does not make our lives happier or better.

► Language influences the way we think; we can change our perceptions by changing the words we use.

► The brain is primed to hold onto negative imagery more than positive imagery.

## HELPFUL THOUGHTS FOR DEALING WITH THE LANGUAGE OF FAILURE

► Write down three recent "fails" of yours. Now rephrase each failure so that there are no negative connotations. Answer this question for each challenge: if there was a gift buried somewhere in this situation, what would it be?

► Avoid using the language of failure to talk to your spouse, children, employees, or employers.

► Consider sending your children to a school that does not give grades or use the language of failure in their report cards.

- ▶ Consider using language that does not result in shaming yourself or anyone else.
- ▶ Below are a few synonyms from the *Collins English Thesaurus*. Which ones have you used recently to describe yourself, someone else, or your actions? How could you change the language you use when speaking of failures such as these? Find words with a positive connotation that could replace these:
    - ▶ Defeat
    - ▶ Disaster
    - ▶ Letdown
    - ▶ Trouble
    - ▶ Tragedy
    - ▶ Misfortune
    - ▶ Devastation
    - ▶ Mishap
    - ▶ Loser
    - ▶ Disappointment
    - ▶ No-good
    - ▶ Flop
    - ▶ Write-off
    - ▶ Incompetent
    - ▶ Washout
    - ▶ Deficient

## NOTES

1. Fenig, Ethel. "President Barack Obama built that." *American Thinker*, November 7, 2013. http://www.americanthinker.com/blog/2013/11/president_barack_obama_built_that.html.

2. "The History of Room 404." Room404.com, 1999. Accessed October 19, 2016. http://www.room404.com/page.php?pg=homepage.

3. "Online Etymology Dictionary." Etymonline.com, 2001. Accessed October 20, 2016. http://www.etymonline.com/index. php?term=fail&allowed_in_frame=0.

4. Syed, *Black Box Thinking*, 69.

5. Ibid., 113.

6. Chengappa, Raj. "Killer exams: How to revamp the system." India Today, March 28, 2005. Accessed March 5, 2017. http://indiatoday.intoday.in/story/growing-number-of-students-commits-suicide-over-exams/1/194023.html.

7. "Explaining the Rise in Youth Suicide." The Anika Foundation, 2014. http://www.anikafoundation.com/rise_in_suicide.shtml.

8. "Suicide by children and young people in England." National Confidential Inquiry into Suicide and Homicide by People with Mental Illness (NCISH). Manchester, UK: University of Manchester Press, 2016. 3. http://research.bmh.manchester. ac.uk/cmhs/research/centreforsuicideprevention/nci/reports/ cyp_report.pdf.

9. DiSalvo, David. "How Language Shapes Our World." Neuronarrrative, April 7, 2009. Accessed March 5, 2017. https://neuronarrative.wordpress.com/2009/04/07/ how-language-shapes-our-world/.

10. Ibid.

11. Marano, Hara Estroff. "Our Brain's Negative Bias." *Psychology Today*, June 20, 2003. Accessed March 5, 2017. https://www. psychologytoday.com/articles/200306/our-brains-negative-bias.

12. Peter Croft. Interview with the authors, December 2016. Name changed for privacy.

# CHAPTER EIGHT

# CHANGING THE NARRATIVE OF FAILURE

I n the groundbreaking book *Healing the Mind through the Power of Story: The Promise of Narrative Psychiatry,* Lewis Mehl-Madrona explores the powerful relationship between the stories we tell ourselves and who we are. In his extensive work with patients who have far-ranging diagnoses from schizophrenia to autism, he cites the making of narrative as a way to transform reality and establish optimum mental health. He says everything, *everything,* is story, and proposes "reinventing psychiatry as the art and science of story. . . . It's all story," he says. "There is nothing but story."[1]

Even science, he claims, is story. The facts that were true yesterday are not true today as new discoveries are made. Textbooks tell different stories about medicine and physics over time. What is fascinating for us—and a building block for this chapter—is what Madrona says about mental illness—schizophrenia, for example. He writes:

> We all have schizophrenic experiences, but most of us call these experiences dreams, daydreams, fantasies, and so on. The person labeled schizophrenic is merely at the extreme of a continuum of being unable to tell the difference between dream and ordinary waking life. He or she can relearn that capacity.[2]

Madrona does exactly this with his patients. He gives them counternarratives. If a patient has been told she is crazy because she is hearing voices and needs medication, he tells her we all hear voices but that she just needs a new story about her voices in order to function better in the world. Through creating counternarratives, he has been able to effectively help many people at the extreme end of a very human continuum.

So what are the societal and individual narratives about failure that we are told and that we tell ourselves? And is it possible that even if we have been living by a narrative that makes us helpless or dysfunctional or depressed, we can be the authors of our own new narratives?

We do, indeed, live by story. Whether the Bible provides us with narratives that guide us, or Hollywood movies, or our corporate workplace ethos, it may help us to identify the narrative we have created about ourselves and look at whether it might need rewriting.

Let's look at some of the narratives that we might live by that talk about failure and success.

"The Prodigal Son" is a puzzling parable. Sometimes known as "The Lost Son" or "The Loving Father," it is a well-known story about failure—about a brilliant fail, really, which runs counter to our dominant cultural narrative in which thoughtless young wasters surely don't deserve to be cut any slack!

Here is a modern interpretation of the parable: a wealthy father divides his estate between his two sons. The first son is frugal and astute and invests the money and assets wisely. The second son, however, is bored with his life at home and has wanderlust. There is also possibly a little twinge of arrogant dismissal of his father's home and parochialism. So he cashes in all his assets and travels the world. Predictably, he soon squanders the money with his wild living and carefree lifestyle and spends every penny without much thought of the future. But the country he now finds himself in is famine ravished and drought stricken, and he soon ends up destitute, hungry, and homeless.

He is lucky to find a job, any job, but it is not a job he would ever have imagined himself doing. He feeds pigs. He is so hungry he wants to eat the pig swill and offal he dishes out to the animals, in spite of the stench. It does not take him long to have his aha moment: *My father's servants have food to spare, and here I am starving to death!* he says to himself. *What am I doing here? I have sunk to the lowest. I would gladly be one of my father's servants at this point. At least I would have enough food and clothing.*

So he swallows his pride and returns to his father's home, rehearsing what to say to him. *Father, I am so sorry. What a fool I've been. I've wasted all your inheritance. I have failed big time. I can't expect you to forgive me, but will you take me as one of your servants? I will gladly work all day for food and shelter.*

But he has no chance to even begin his speech, for when he is still a long way off, his father runs to him, kisses him, and welcomes him home. "Quick, give the boy some decent clothes," he tells his servants. "And let him shower; he smells like pig swill. And feed him, he's starving, the poor boy."

And so that night, the father throws a party, brings out his best wine and food, and celebrates the return of his long-lost son. "I thought you were dead!" he says.

The ending is disquieting and uncomfortable because it messes with assumptions many of us may have about who deserves to be rewarded and who deserves to be treated as a loser. *Hang on—didn't this guy just fail? What is he being rewarded for? Wasting money, time, talent? Failing?*

And this is exactly what his brother, the brooding first son, thinks. He comes home after a hard day's work and hears music and drunken laughter, sees a crackling barbecue, smells a delicious roast. When he sees his younger brother at the centre, he gets jealous.

He pulls his father aside. "What is this?"

"Your brother has returned. Come join us and celebrate."

"You're kidding, right? I've been the best steward of your property for all those years he was frittering away your money. I haven't squandered anything. I have been a true son. And you never threw a party for me. What is going on here?"

"My son," the father says, "you are always with me, and everything I have is yours. But your brother was lost, and now he's found. Aren't you happy he's back?"

The moral of the story is that the second son (the failure, the bum, the ungrateful one) is the one who has made a journey of some kind, experienced things not turning out as he had hoped (failure), and is a wiser person for it. He has learned something. The first son has remained static, has not learned the lessons of loss, pain, and, therefore, appreciation.

The message of the story? The so-called failure leads to realisation. The journey, the experience of failure, is valuable in that it leads to enlightenment about what is valuable in life, and the father recognises his son's transformation.

What we term "failure," as stated in previous chapters, is part of life. It's part of our narrative. It's a necessary and vital step on the journey to self-realisation, regardless of the destination. Being wrong, experiencing the unanticipated outcomes, and acknowledging our falls and stumbles are all keys to growth.

Most of us have been prodigal sons at one point in our lives. We have all taken wrong turns, made mistakes, been inadequate, not achieved what we believe is our potential, not lived up to our own expectations, not fulfilled our dreams. We might wish we could go back on some disastrous decisions we have made, even some minor ones that have led us down a path that is the equivalent of living in pig swill. Sometimes we may not feel like better people because of it either. We might wish we could now return home and be forgiven, be welcomed by our father and have the errors, the "failures," wiped away. But in real life, that does not always happen. Some people have to live with pretty significant challenges. You marry a person who makes your life a misery. You have an illegitimate child and, without money, have to live with your parents. You lose your job and cannot find another one. These situations are real, and they affect most of us at one time or another.

But the crucial thing is: what we do with our stories? How do we view them when they don't have the happy outcome we want?

J.K. Rowling tells her rags-to-riches story and makes sense of her early "failure" as a stepping stone to her unimaginable success.

We can look at our own stories and create counternarratives using the exact same facts demonstrated in the previous chapter. In Chapter Seven, we looked at the language of failure and how words shape our reality. In this chapter, we look at the narrative of failure and its role in our lives. "The Prodigal Son" tells us that failure teaches us not how to *succeed* but how to *appreciate* what we took for granted.

We can embrace that plotline and apply it to our own lives if we want to.

Most of us are affected, at least to some degree, by Hollywood stories—it's not a multibillion-dollar industry for nothing. We are addicted to story, and we are prepared to pay for it. The fact that we even say "Hollywood ending" means we know exactly what that is. We crave the happily ever after and go to see repetitive movies over and over because they provide us with narrative structures that make us feel hopeful about our own lives. Hollywood movies are mostly about success, with failure as a temporary setback.

# SUCCESSFUL FAILURE

The classic Hollywood narrative of failure insists on a successful fairy-tale ending. *Back to the Future*[3] is exactly what we wish for: an opportunity for Marty McFly to undo the failure of his and his parents' lives and to turn that failure into success. The present McFly family has failed: Uncle Joey is in prison, Marty is not recognised as a musician and is a "slacker" at school, his parents are losers, the bully Biff has the upper hand, and Marty fears that his pattern of failure is genetic. "No McFly amounted to anything in the history of Hill Valley" is the mantra that plagues him. He is a failure and is doomed to be a failure forever. Such is life. We identify with it because this is a realistic picture of the majority of the world's population.

But "things are going to change." By returning to the past, Marty can undo the failures of his parents, defeat Biff, and create a successful future.

What do we do with this fairy-tale ending we love so much? We believe in such fairy-tale endings. We want to believe in the American dream, articulated by McFly: "You can achieve anything if you set your mind to it."[4]

The myth or fairy tale does not originate in Hollywood. It is ingrained in us over thousands of years of myths, stories, and hero legends. Joseph Campbell documented them, synthesized them, and came up with a formula of a singular Hero myth that is common to all cultures: In the narrative of *The Hero with a Thousand Faces*,[5] which feels embedded in our human DNA, the hero sets out on a journey. Something is wrong: his society has failed or he has failed, and he has to set it right. He gets help, fails again, passes thresholds, wins a small battle but then fails epically, and finally, when all is near lost, he succeeds in defeating the evil enemy, or returning with the gold, or healing himself or his society.[6]

This is a failure-to-success story that we believe in as though it is a fact. We watch it on TV and in movies, we read it, dream it, try to apply it to our lives, applaud when we see instances of it in real life. It is an evolutionary story about evolving into better human beings and defeating the darkness of our bad karma.

Hollywood has used this formula over and over again because it works. We identify with the hero and turn our lives into a quest to succeed and overcome failure. This is why we love Zusak or Rowling—they are heroes, and we believe we can be like them.

But that is one narrative. What about the other stories, the millions of stories where the prodigal son cannot return home?

An intriguing poem by Elizabeth Bishop gives us an ironic but moving narrative on loss. In her poem "One Art," she writes that "the art of losing isn't hard to master." Bishop's narrator makes the point that losing things is an easy skill to acquire and that it is not a disaster to fail. However, the poignant undertone of the poem tells a different story: she is not so sure that failure isn't a disaster. She loses things, then houses, even continents, and finally the person she loves most in the world. And that final loss, which she resists admitting, feels to her "like disaster." Her point is that failure, loss, the unanticipated are all narratives of our lives just as the Hollywood hero myth is: we lose things, we regret things, we fail, and we have no choice in the end but to find ways to go with the flow and accept the things we cannot change.[7]

In 2008, Gerry and Martha Hutchinson[8] emigrated to Australia from the third world. They had very little money and could not afford to buy a house—house prices in Australia were among the highest in the world. But they stumbled on a magnificent Queenslander to rent—the traditional two-storey homestead with wraparound verandas, chandeliers, a large swimming pool, and Italian marble statues dotted around the two acres of lush botanical gardens. The rent was miraculously low. As they earned more and more money, they were now in a position to buy a house, but they could not afford such a house as they were renting, as it was worth over $700,000. The owners, however, said they could have it for $600,000. The Hutchinsons could not afford $600,000 and countered at $550,000. The owners refused that offer, and the realtor made it clear that she wanted them out so she could sell the house to "real" buyers.

So they left and found a small house to buy without a pool or large rooms or high ceilings in a not-so-nice area. They were heartbroken to leave but realised their limitations. They could never have afforded such a luxury house. It was out of their league. For two years, though, they had lived and felt like millionaires.

A few months later, however, they saw that the Queenslander had sold to someone else for exactly $550,000, and they called the realtor in shock. "Well, the owner had many, many low offers and decided to sell up for $550,000—so you could have had the house if you had stuck around."

It was unfair. They could have had that house. But it was a failure—one they regretted and could never recover from, because soon after this, house prices rose sharply and a house of that size would sell now for over $800,000.

The lesson they tried to learn was that they had not appreciated what they had, they had missed an opportunity which would never come again. They were like prodigal sons who had foolishly left what they had but now could not return. And unlike the proverb with the happy ending, there was no welcoming realtor saying, "All is forgiven—you can have your house back. Welcome home!" This was the ending of their house story, and they had to live with that.

Many of us experience such lost opportunities or misjudgements, and we cannot go back and fix them. We regret certain decisions or indecisions. In real life, sons cannot always return to Papa and have a happy ending. We lose things. Relationships fail, and we cannot ever have back what we did not appreciate.

The important thing, as we have been trying to show, is how we deal with these outcomes we call failures. Is there a counternarrative that could reframe our stories so that we aren't trapped in a binary world of success and failure?

Another example of the son who cannot return home is a Hollywood TV series from the sixties, *Lost in Space*.[9] *Lost in Space* is the story of the Robinson family who sets off to explore the new frontier of outer space. But very soon on their journey, a Russian spy, Dr. Smith, sabotages the mission and leaves them "lost in space," drifting forever, never able to return to Earth or accomplish their mission. Their story is that of colossal failure, lurching in each episode from one disastrous adventure to another. This is a series that celebrates failure, or at least acknowledges its value in creating conflict and surprising outcomes that are not linear, not the hero's journey. They have to make do, camp on inhospitable planets, and live with their failure—including having to live in close confines with the obnoxious Dr. Smith, who continues to disrupt and spoil their plans. Instead of vanquishing the enemy and killing him, restoring order, and achieving a happy Hollywood ending, they have to reconcile with the enemy. This more realistic portrayal of what actually happens in people's lives is refreshing. For most of us, our lives do not go as planned: we fail, and we have to live with the consequences of our actions—or the consequences of other people's actions on us. Life is not a hero's journey for most of us. *Lost in Space* is about how to live with failure, with things not working out as planned.

## LIVING WITH FAILURE

The Hutchinsons in our Queenslander story had to come to live with the loss of their house. They regretted it, missed it, beat themselves up over it, but had to make friends with failure. How? They had several options:

1. They could regret it, grow bitter, feed the narrative of themselves as bumbling failures.
2. They could live with failure as a normal part of life—an irritant, a reminder of all they lost, but one that spurs them on to keep going.
3. They could use their failure as a lesson in acquiring insight and wisdom.
4. They could reframe the narrative. *Is it really failure? If failure is a normal part of human life, then why diminish it? We accept that these are challenges life throws our way.*

In the end, they spent time in each one of these narratives. They realised this was not a first-degree failure—even though in the beginning, the pain of the loss overrode almost every other thought and feeling. Most recently, they could say that the most helpful narrative was the last one. They tell this story to themselves:

"This kind of thing is just life. It happened, and we don't have the power to go back and rewrite the actual events. We're not going to demonise the event or ourselves. We have the power to make NOW as full of joy and appreciation as possible. Let's just do it."[10]

Milan Kundera begins his novel *The Unbearable Lightness of Being*[11] with a discussion about reincarnation. The prospect of eternal return, he argues, is an attractive one because we get a chance to undo the mistakes we made in our first life, and have a second, or even third and fourth, attempt to get it right. But if we live only once, we cannot be too hard on ourselves if we fail, because we have not been this way before.

There are other narratives, too, that we have lived by: while the Ancient Greeks (and Joseph Campbell) presented a hero myth as a life narrative, they also presented us with a twin-faced tragedy/comedy myth. In the comedy myth, all's well that ends well, and similar to the hero myth, the hero fixes up the flaws of his or her society and everyone except the villain lives happily ever after. Look at any Shakespeare comedy or modern romantic comedy to see this narrative in operation. In this story, all errors are simply misunderstandings and can be put right at the end. *Pretty Woman*[12] is a case in point. The 1990 movie starring Julia Roberts as a prostitute who turns into a "princess" has warmed millions of hearts because of its fairy-tale plot and happy ending. It is a rags-to-riches narrative that feeds and confirms our belief in "happily ever after." Nice, but not everyone's reality.

It is the other Greek narrative, tragedy, that deals with failure in a more realistic way.

## TRAGIC FAILURE

Many of us studied Arthur Miller's *Death of a Salesman*[13] at school or college and hated it. Why? Because it is about failure, defeat, tragedy, and suicide. Things do not go well for Willy Loman, or Biff and Happy, or Willy's wife. It is not a Hollywood ending—it is about failure as a terminal illness.

What if the prodigal son makes all his mistakes and his father does not welcome him home?

The Greeks delineated a counternarrative to comedy in which failure triumphed and never was vanquished: tragedy. Oedipus Rex mistakenly kills his father and marries his mother, and his whole kingdom falls into ruin until he kills himself. Any Shakespearean tragedy follows the same formula: a great man has a flaw and, through stupid decisions, falls from grace and loses everything.

Why would we want to uphold a narrative like that?

Well, because maybe we can get something from it. The Greeks called it catharsis: purification or cleansing, letting go of the negative emotions inside us. By experiencing the narrative of tragedy on stage, secondhand, we can be purged of the grief inside us. A great man has to be sacrificed for the common good. But no one wants to be that failed person. We want to benefit from the failure, not be the failure.

Guy de Maupassant's "The Necklace"[14] is a short story about a proud, vain, young French woman who borrows a million-dollar diamond necklace to go to a ball, loses it, and spends the rest of her life paying it off. Unknown to her until the end, the diamond necklace was fake and valueless, which meant that her suffering was pointless and her whole life was not only a failure but absurdly meaningless.

But there is a moral to the story. If she had not been so vain, she would have swallowed her pride and told the truth to the person who loaned her the necklace and would never have gone through the tragic suffering. Her story could so easily have been different, but she rigidly believed it to be fixed in stone.

If we question the narratives we take as solidly factual, then maybe we can find the counternarrative, one which will enable us to avoid tragedy.

Paul, the coauthor of this book, is best friends with failure. He spent many years trying to succeed at various careers, and each endeavour ended in failure. He realised that he was a success at one thing—failure—and decided to turn this experience into a humorous job application and send it to a literary journal as a short story.

## APPLICATION FOR POSITION AS FAILURE

Dear Sir/Madam,

I wish to apply for the position you advertised in the *Daily Sun*. Although my expertise is in self-obliteration and self-worth (or lack of), and my work mainly in disappointment, I do have much experience in failure, which this letter will strive to illustrate.

Please find below a brief summary of my work experience.

I have been a failure since I was four years old. From the very start, I was ambitious and set my hopes high. I wanted too much out of life and consequently came short. I wanted to be somebody and became nobody.

My early career aspirations were lofty: writer, film-maker, movie star, musician. I have been a consistent failure at each. My first love was film. All through my childhood, I played out cowboy-and-Indian battles in my head; I sketched out intricate plots of murder mysteries where the murderer hid behind shadows of shadows of other characters; I ran and reran in my head (complete with soundtrack) wild adventures in darkest Africa; I acted out scenes of survivors clawing up endless sand dunes to reach imaginary oases. I was brimming with ideas. I spent weeks and months and years making plasticene frame-by-frame animations of little space creatures on Mars. I sent off proposals to Hollywood, grant proposals to Disney, samples to Tisch School of the Arts in New York. I aspired; I dreamed. I was destined to be the next Lucas, Spielberg, Goddard. It had to happen, I thought, because I believed it so strongly.

It didn't.

A strong component of failure is the willingness to try again and again. It is the belief in success that gives me the edge in this regard.

At twelve, I learned to play the guitar, keyboard, drums. I was going to be the next Hendrix, Santana, Bon Jovi. Behind closed bedroom doors, I mimed my way through teenage-hood to Nirvana, eyes closed, headphones clamped to my head, in front of imaginary crowds cheering and screaming girls wetting their pants. I made it into a school band, but at the first and last Battle of the Bands competition I played in, we came dead last.

Most of all, I wanted to be a bestselling author, a paperback writer, a Nobel Prize winner. I spent my university days writing out plot summaries, listing titles of books I would write, discussing literature with other would-be writers in clouds of cigarette smoke. All through my twenties, I wrote novels, none of which are complete and none of which have been published. I submitted them to over two hundred publishers. I wrote for every competition imaginable; I sliced off pieces of my soul at each attempt. Each rejection was a blow to an already over-bruised soul.

I was close once. Black Bird Publishers wanted to see my novel called *Fail!* (about a failed writer) and suggested I rewrite it. I rewrote it. *Can you change the title and the main character? Make him more . . . positive?* Sure. *And the ending more upbeat?* Of course. *Less of a loser?* Sure, sure. Ultimately, however, they had to reject it, calling it a critical failure. (I enclose the letter for your perusal in lieu of a letter of recommendation, which they would not give me.)

I enclose no other letters of recommendation. Unfortunately, all those I approached did not get back to me—or those who did couldn't remember who I was or what I had achieved.

My experience is deep and broad and painful. For those who say "Failure is not an option" and then fail, the caverns they carve in their own flesh are huge. Let no one say I have lived a shallow life. My wounds go deep.

As for my personal life, my relationships have been consistently dysfunctional. I fell in love many times, and never once has love been reciprocated, except on rare occasions when my partner sought to exploit me for whatever reason or to use me for some self-aggrandizing project of her own. My first love was a girl called Denise (thirteen), but being too tongue tied and inept at fourteen, I watched her affection grow cold and finally shrink to nothing as she walked off with my best friend into a private sunset of their own. My nearest approximation of success—I could smell it—was when I met a model whom I courted and wooed online. She invited me to LA. I flew on intercontinental Virgin wings, arrived with expensive bottles of wine and nervous plans of seduction and lifelong romance, but at that first meeting—she could smell failure—she informed me that a new boyfriend had somehow materialized and that I could stay as long as I wanted as long as I didn't come anywhere near her.

Academically, I have taken the less-travelled road. I rose to the ranks of graduate assistant, and then in lieu of a PhD, I took on the mantle of failed academic. I was always snubbed by sharper critics and felt dull and slow in their presence.

Applying for jobs brought me a sea of rejection slips to rival my writing failures. Finally I was begrudgingly given a temporary position at a second-rate business firm (ranked 2421 out of 2423 in *Forbes* magazine) because the person they wanted to hire was unavailable and I was a temporary stand-in. I was a ghost, never seen, never given an office—no one remembered my name or what I was doing there. In time, the permanent position became available: I applied for it, and it was given to a young graduate with large front teeth (not that I have anything against large front teeth).

My patron saint is St. Jude.

Failure, of course, is only measurable by aspiration: I wanted to be an athletic stud; a brilliant mind; a creative, famous writing personality; a movie star, someone who everyone would whisper after and say "There he is!"; a musician of exceptional talent who pioneered a new wave of sound. As a filmmaker too, I could have performed artistic miracles. But . . . but . . . I have instead a resume filled with regret.

My soul has taken a battering, and if it were visible, you would see the scars, the marks of history. Like a sponge, it absorbs the poison of society and now is officially disabled. It hobbles in wary scepticism; my optimism has been scuffed; the shape of failure shadows me everywhere: I have a perpetual psychological limp.

Would you be interested in such a person? I am large enough to continue brightly without hope and idealistic enough to march into more pain.

I have the energy, the drive, the blackness in me to try and try again. Out of desperation. I refuse to go down in history as a Nobody who did Nothing.

I look forward to hearing from you if you are interested in my application (which I know you won't be, but I'm ever hopeful . . .)

Thank you for your consideration.

Yours truly.[15]

The irony: Paul submitted this story to every journal he thought would be interested. It was rejected by all of them. Failure obviously was not a good topic!

But for Paul, writing the story-letter, making failure a subject, became his catharsis. The act of creativity helped him get an ironic perspective on his perceived shortcomings and his idea of failure. He stopped taking himself so seriously.

Soon after the last rejection of the failure story, he landed a job teaching English at a university. His short stories began to get published, and he could use this failure story as a path-to-success story.

Maybe the only freedom we really have is in the story that we tell ourselves, the narratives we create around the events in our lives. If stories shape our lives, we have the power to change the narratives and retell the story of our failure and successes. It is in our power to change the way we perceive our past, present, and future.

## BIG IDEAS

► Everything is story: our lives are profoundly influenced by our choice of narrative.

► Stories shape us: "The Prodigal Son" highlights that learning compassion, empathy, and appreciation is a valuable achievement in itself, despite failing at life.

► We expect our lives to follow the trajectory of the hero's journey, and we are then devastated when they don't.

► We often aren't conscious that we are influenced by a societal narrative in which failure-to-success makes for the only acceptable plotline.

► Writing counternarratives frees us to be honest and empowered about how we tackle the present.

## HELPFUL THOUGHTS ON CREATING COUNTER-FAILURE NARRATIVES

We are free to look at our setbacks in life in any way. Here are some suggestions:

► **Hero's journey strategy:** See a setback as part of the journey, as something to overcome.

- ► **Tragic hero's strategy:** Acknowledge the pattern: identify the flaw, and understand what led to it in the first place. Maybe there are lessons to be learned; maybe not.
- ► *Lost in Space* **strategy:** Accept what cannot be undone; don't blame yourself for the outcome. We do not have a time machine to fix the past, so don't beat yourself up over it.
- ► Make the best of the present moment and reframe the failure narrative.
- ► "I always fail" means you are programming yourself. Is it really failure at all? The way forward is to tell a new story, building on the ideas put forward in Chapter Seven.

## NOTES

1. Mehl-Madrona, Lewis. *Healing the Mind through the Power of Story: The Promise of Narrative Psychiatry.* Rochester, VT: Bear & Company, 2010. 2.
2. Ibid., 8.
3. *Back to The Future.* Directed by Robert Zemeckis. Universal City, CA: Universal Pictures, 1985.
4. Elsaesser, Thomas, and Warren Buckland. *Studying Contemporary American Film: A Guide to Movie Analysis.* London: Bloomsbury Academic, 2002. 234.
5. Campbell, Joseph. *The Hero with a Thousand Faces.* Novato, CA: New World Library, 2008.
6. "Hero's Journey." Wikipedia. Accessed January 23, 2017. https://en.wikipedia.org/wiki/Hero's_journey.
7. Bishop, Elizabeth. "One Art." In *The Complete Poems: 1927–1979.* New York: Farrar, Straus and Giroux, 1983.
8. Gerry and Martha Hutchinson. Interview with the authors, 2016. Names changed for privacy.
9. *Lost in Space.* Century City, CA: CBS, 1967.
10. Hutchinson, interview.

11. Kundera, Milan. *The Unbearable Lightness of Being*. New York: Harper Perennial Modern Classics, 2005.

12. *Pretty Woman*. Directed by Garry Marshall. Los Angeles: Touchstone Pictures and Silver Screen Partners IV, 1990.

13. Miller, Arthur. *Death of a Salesman*. New York: Morosco Theater, 1949.

14. De Maupassant, Guy. "The Necklace." *Le Galois*, February 17, 1884.

15. Williams, Paul. "Application for Position of Failure." 2017. Unpublished.

# CHAPTER NINE

# PHILOSOPHIES OF FAILURE

I n this chapter, we will explore different philosophical worldviews and how they deal with failure. There isn't a "right" view, nor is there one that will work for everyone. Some of these worldviews may make perfect sense to you; others you may scoff at. This chapter doesn't aim to provide you with an answer for how to deal with failure; there isn't one philosophy that can do that for everyone. Instead, we give you different views, different tools that you can examine and experiment with, as well as an overview so you can see where your particular worldview fits with others.

Every single story we tell ourselves about failure and every point of view we have about failure has its roots far back in time. Our responses, our narratives about so-called failure, are largely determined by our worldview, our philosophy of life. Failure has been a topic of discussion amidst philosophers since philosophy's early beginnings in Ancient Greece, China, and India around 400 BCE.

# SPIRITUAL WORLDVIEWS

## BUDDHISM

Buddhism originated in India sometime between the sixth and fourth centuries BCE. Buddhism maintains that the desire to succeed and escape failure is itself the problem, and if we cease to desire, then we will be content with ourselves. As mentioned in Chapter Four, Buddhism is founded on the Four Noble Truths, the First of these that life is suffering. It is impossible to live without experiencing failure, unhappiness, physical illness, injury, old age, and eventually death as well as psychological suffering. Life will inevitably fail to live up to our expectations of it. The Second Noble Truth, however, states that the cause of this suffering is desire: our very expectation that life should be successful causes our unhappiness. The need for more, for fulfilment and satisfaction, is not a bad thing—it is our primal drive, a survival instinct—but it keeps us unhappy and makes us see our lives as failures.

The Third and Fourth Noble Truths provide the solution: to practise not being attached to stuff, to stop desiring, is the only way to alleviate our suffering.

Failure is only a manufactured lack of success, and success is an illusion. In light of this worldview, we should acknowledge that our desire to win, to succeed, is probably the very thing that is making us unhappy.

Wanting what we can't or might not have does tend to cause us distress. This example highlights the point that the Buddhists make about how we cause ourselves pain:

Harry and June Webster[1] were married twenty years ago. They had an idealistic view of their lives together. They planned to work hard and eventually be wealthy, have a beautiful house, raise three children, and live happy lives. Their married life began well, their first child was born healthy, they purchased the house of their dreams. But as life would have it, Harry lost his well-paid job, and they had to downsize to a poky apartment. June could not have more children due to a medical condition, and they began to resent their ill fortune, mourn what they had lost. They began most sentences with "If only" or "It should have been." They lived very unhappy lives, holding that picture of their ideal life as a comparison to how their life was now. Instead of being grateful for the life they had—a beautiful, healthy child; an apartment near the beach; two jobs which, while not spectacular, afforded them enough money to live on—they felt their lives were a failure because their lived reality did not match the ideal picture they had created. The desire for an imagined life spoiled their enjoyment of the life they had.

We often blind ourselves and disregard our present by calling it a failure because it falls short of our idealised picture or our desires. This approach belongs to those who are blinded to the successes they have because of some imagined or alternative success they desire. Desire in this case creates a sense of failure.

It took a tragic turn of events for Harry and June to realise what they had and to learn to appreciate their successes and stop labelling them as failures. A life-threatening illness made them see how blessed their lives were, how fortunate their situation was, and how hard they had worked to achieve success.

## ANCIENT GREECE: PLATO'S ALLEGORY OF THE CAVE

In his "Allegory of the Cave," the Greek philosopher Plato (fourth century BCE) shows how the physical world is simply an illusion, a reality constructed for us by some conspiracy elite who keep us enthralled by images and fool us into thinking that this is the real world. This allegory was written more than two thousand years before movies and television (380–360 BCE), yet there's a powerful message here, as if Plato predicted the impact of media-induced images on our perception of reality.

Here is a summary of the allegory:

Down in the deepest parts of the earth, there is a cave. In this cave, people live, but they are chained to each other and to a rock. They stand in a row at the back of the cave and watch a show of shadows on the cave wall. Puppeteers manipulate the images, using a fire to cast the shadows. They control what the enslaved people see. To the people who have known nothing else, these shadows are reality. They believe in the shadows because that is all they are shown. But then, one day, a man escapes his chains. He creeps out of the cave and heads upwards, drawn by a force he cannot name. After some time, he emerges out of the cave and steps into the world. He feels the full, bright light of the sun on his eyes. At first, he is blinded. Then, as his eyes adjust, he comes to see a magnificent world of colour and light and beauty. He realises with horror that what he thought was real his whole life is only a shadow of the actual thing. Up until now, he has only seen copies of certain objects, but now that he has escaped the cave into the light and sees the world, he notes that these trees, this sky, these animals and people are the "real" things. Inspired, overwhelmed, he returns to the cave. He is burning to tell everyone that their world is all illusion, that the real thing is out there, if only they will follow him. At first, they simply laugh at him. Then, when he gets too insistent, they put him to death for threatening the status quo.

It is a bizarre allegory but one we can all relate to. These days, virtual reality and powerful media—our modern "caves"—constitute the "reality" of many people's lives. We chase after those shadows as if they are real and lose connection with nature, other real humans, and fresh air and sunlight!

Plato's theory is the basis for a worldview that has been around longer than any other and is the centre of most religious belief systems: the world is not real. It is flawed. It is a bad copy of the real thing, which is elsewhere, outside of this one, on a spiritual plane.

So how does this relate to failure? According to Plato, our yearning for success, for perfection, is doomed to fail, because we are in a cave, tied to the things and images of our own making. We have to stop chasing after the shadows and thinking they are real, because they aren't.

The Platonists among us, who include any believers in all the major religions, believe that the physical world is imperfect by its very nature, and so whatever people try to achieve will never reach perfection in this life. We can strive and improve, but ultimately the consolation is that failure is built in. We will fail, we will not achieve, and we will die. The hope we have is that there is more than this imperfect life.

The novelist Cormac McCarthy (author of such books as *The Road*, *All the Pretty Horses*, and *No Country for Old Men*) gave a rare interview with Oprah Winfrey where he describes himself as a Platonist when it comes to writing novels:

> You always have this image of the perfect thing which you can never achieve, but which you never stop trying to achieve . . . That's your signpost and your guide. You can't plot things out. You just have to trust in, you know, wherever it comes from.[2]

Seeing the material world and all its struggles and failures as shadows on the wall of a cave enables us to detach from it and see it as a flurry of transience that is less important than the Real, the spiritual world. Plato's Cave gives us perspective.

# MATERIALIST WORLDVIEWS

### ROMAN PHILOSOPHIES AND THE ART OF FAILING WISELY

In contrast to Platonic, Idealist philosophies of life and corresponding religious worldviews, the Hellenistic philosophies of Stoicism and Epicureanism provide a different attitude to failure. These two philosophies have carried through to modern thinking: the Romans sought practical ways to live life, and these philosophical views were regarded as an art.

## EPICUREANISM

Epicurus (circa 341–270 BCE) was a materialist who disagreed with Plato's ideal world of forms and did not believe in the Gods, divine intervention, or a dualistic universe where the spiritual world took preference over the material one. For Epicurus, the attainment of pleasure in this life was the highest good. That pleasure came through obtaining freedom from fear—what he called *ataraxia*—and bodily pain—*aponia*. Epicureanism advocates we should aim for a life free from fear and pain. This was enough to give us happiness.

Epicurus argued for an "imperturbability," or a measured appreciation of what we do have, that we needed to cultivate an "undisturbable" quality or disposition or frame of mind. Like the Buddhists, he argued that we are miserable because we desire and crave what we do not—cannot—have. So if we can be content with how things are, the natural state of things, rather than seeing our lives as a failing of one sort of another, we can bathe in the "pure joy of being" and take pleasure in our existence.[3]

An Epicurean view on life, then, is not to discount reality and imperfection and failure as being part of a realm of shadows or to believe in a perfect ideal outside of this material world but to live humbly and simply, avoiding or minimising fear and pain. Failure, then, is evident only if we don't manage to keep our fear and pain at bay.

## STOICISM

Stoicism, another Roman philosophy of life, is described in modern thinking as a "grin and bear it" philosophy, a fatalistic acceptance of life's hardships. If we call someone a "stoic," we admire (or maybe do not admire) their ability to endure hardship, adversity, and failure. In contrast to Epicureans, Stoics believe that many things are not in our control and failure is the norm: ill health, death, and loss of loved ones, property, or wealth are all realities we need to face. We are all subject to this type of failure. All we can do is accept the inevitability of fate's capriciousness. In Stoicism, there is no God, but there is life, and it is not fair. Our best bet lies in recognising that life is mostly not under our control. We need courage to endure, accept, and understand how life is.

Seneca, the Roman Stoic, advised us to learn the art of failing wisely by a measured acceptance of the inability to succeed as par for the course: "Nothing happens to the wise man contrary to his expectation."4

The Stoics practised "negative visualisation"—anticipating what could go wrong, the worst-case scenario, what was outside their control. Sometimes this is a good strategy if we wish to avoid disappointment. Expect failure. But resignation need not be negative. Resignation means accepting that this world is made of failure, that it is how the world works. It is not a perfect world. We ultimately fail by dying; we deteriorate, get diseases—and whatever ideal we hold, we need to recognize that the yearning for perfection will always result in failure.

# BIBLICAL WORLDVIEWS AND FAILURE

## OLD TESTAMENT PHILOSOPHIES

The story of Job is often held up as an example of someone who never loses faith despite overwhelming adversity. This is a story that, for Judeo-Christian believers, lends itself to the philosophy that there is meaning behind suffering—even if we don't understand it. Job is a righteous man who becomes a pawn in a wager between God and Satan. The Torah and the Old Testament tell the story of this wealthy man, favoured by God, who was tested to the limits. God allowed everything to go wrong in Job's life: he lost his house, fortune, wife, health, and respect. In other words, his life became an epic fail. But still he would not curse God and instead accepted his lot. This was the test: would Job lose faith and give in to depression and blame God, curse his fate, and wish to die?

Nearly. But Job kept his worldview intact. If God wanted him to suffer and lose everything, then who was he to complain? So he passed the "test," and God won the wager against Satan. In the end, God gave him back everything and more, but the point of the story is that he did not give up because of his failures. The lesson here? Accept God's will. This is how it is. Don't wish for a better life or regret your losses. In this framework, God has a reason for throwing these things your way and you will be rewarded at the end.

In other words, fail gracefully! If the ground collapses underneath you, don't fight it and clutch at the grass edges; let yourself fall down the chute. We hear many stories of babies who survive falls from balconies not because they are resilient or psychically prepared but because they are relaxed and unaware of the danger, as opposed to adults who tense and anticipate and steel themselves against the worst outcome.[5, 6]

We all know people who grow bitter when bad things happen to them and blame themselves, others, and God or fate, unaccepting of what life has thrown at them. And we all know people who we admire because of the gracious way they accept adversity rather than rail against it. Paul's father, for example, was diagnosed with terminal cancer a few years back. Instead of despairing, resenting those who were healthy, or cursing God, he decided to make the most of the years remaining of his life and began to be kind to people, writing letters asking for forgiveness from those he had harmed. There was no happy reprieve for him, but he died peacefully and in harmony with his friends and relatives.

Things ended well for Job, but even if they hadn't, his attitude can still be valuable to those who do not live within a religious or spiritual framework. Job did not know he was going to be rewarded. *This is life*, he said. And what happened to Job happens to a lot of us. We lose our jobs, our houses, our relationships, our health. We don't know if we're going to see light at the end of the tunnel. Instead of raging against God or fate or ourselves, blaming everyone ("Why did this have to happen to me?") or ourselves ("I am so stupid; I can't believe I did this!"), the story gives us permission to let go, accept everything, be grateful for what we do have, and appreciate what we had before, with the idea that if we do this with as much grace as Job, we may have it again.

## NEW TESTAMENT PHILOSOPHIES

The Bible and other religious texts tell us that God created the universe to run a certain way but that Satan entered it and ruined everything, so that all that we do will result in more and more failure. We have an idea of how things should be, but they are not like that. Why, for example, should we age and die? Why should we suffer? Why do disasters (first-degree failures) occur? The Bible explains why things go wrong, why there is death, pain, suffering, etc. The physical world has fallen into sin and is doomed to failure. We need to simply accept the fact that the world is in a failed state. This will help us realise why things go wrong. But if we are believers, religious texts tell us that there is indeed a happy ending: God has made provision to end the failure and to ultimately redeem his creation, and so if we follow the right path and his laws, then we can have that happy ending too. In this model, there is an underlying moral law to the universe that helps us make sense of things. Of course, the happy ending does not truly occur in this life but in the next.

An often-quoted verse in the New Testament sets up the philosophical premise about how we can overcome all failure: "We know that all things work together for good, for those who love God, who are called according to his purpose." (Romans 8:28, NRSV). In other words, everything that happens to you is part of a grand design, a plan to help you succeed, even if only in the Afterlife. Failure has a meaning—it is part of the rocky road to success in the long run. Providing we trust in God, have faith, and follow Him, then we can turn all the misfortunes and failures into learning experiences that make us better people. There is a Plan, and nothing that happens in our lives or in the world is arbitrary or meaningless.

This is a comforting philosophy because it gives us an explanation for everything that goes wrong in our lives. For example, if we live according to this philosophical point of view and our car breaks down on the way to see a friend, we reason that God meant for this to happen so that we might meet the stranger who gave us help or learn patience or courage.

When we lose jobs, when we "fail" or make mistakes and take wrong turns, we will look at these as moral trials, tests, learning experiences; this underpins many positive views of seeing failure as a teacher. What can we learn from this to make us better people? In the case of first-degree failures, although we cannot understand them, we accept that somehow they are all part of God's plan and we should not despair or lose faith.

But what if we do not have these beliefs? This philosophical worldview is still a useful framework even if you do not subscribe to this particular religious worldview because it contextualises second- and third-degree failures as something positive. This is the philosophy that may lie behind the stories that look for the silver lining in failures of our own making. Even first-degree failures can be seen as part of some larger picture we do not understand; it impels us to keep positive about our lives, trust that we can find some good in this, use this setback as a character-building exercise, and grow our spiritual resilience against adversity.

# MODERN PHILOSOPHIES OF EXISTENTIALISM AND THE ABSURD

Existentialism is a philosophy that emerged in late-nineteeth- and twentieth-century Europe. It maintains that out of the meaninglessness and apparent absurdity of the world, we have to make meaning of our lives. It urges us to live positively and more authentically in the light of death, failure, and bleak nihilism.

For the existentialist, the starting point of a more authentic life is the realisation that life is absolutely meaningless, absurd, and chaotic. There is no God or intelligent design. There is no organising system to help us make sense of life. Everything is heading towards entropy and dissolution. There is no plan. We should shed our "bad faith" (idealistic, inauthentic, unexamined worldviews) and live life passionately and sincerely. We should be realists.

This worldview meets us everywhere today. Costica Bradatan argues in his *New York Times* article "In Praise of Failure" that failure is a necessary step in self-actualisation in an absurd world:

> Failure is the sudden irruption of nothingness into the midst of existence. To experience failure is to start seeing the cracks in the fabric of being, and that's precisely the moment when, properly digested, failure turns out to be a blessing in disguise. For it is this lurking, constant threat that should make us aware of the extraordinariness of our being: the miracle that

we exist at all when there is no reason that we should. Knowing that gives us some dignity.

In this role, failure also possesses a distinct *therapeutic* function. Most of us (the most self-aware or enlightened excepted) suffer chronically from a poor adjustment to existence; we compulsively fancy ourselves much more important than we are and behave as though the world exists only for our sake; in our worst moments, we place ourselves like infants at the center of everything and expect the rest of the universe to be always at our service. We insatiably devour other species, denude the planet of life, and fill it with trash. Failure could be a medicine against such arrogance and hubris, as it often brings humility.[7]

The existentialist philosopher Jean-Paul Sartre would agree. "All human actions," he maintains, "are equivalent and all are on principle doomed to failure,"[8] and "the absurd is the failure of the world to satisfy human expectations of it."[9] But by taking this worldview, we choose to live consciously, shed our bad faith, and create a meaning for our lives.

Albert Camus, the major proponent of the philosophy of the Absurd, uses the Ancient Greek myth of Sisyphus to illustrate his philosophy. In the myth, as a punishment for disobeying the gods, Sisyphus has to push a huge rock up a hill. When he gets to the top, the rock rolls down to the bottom and he has to roll it up again.

Forever.

Camus wonders what goes through the poor man's mind as he performs this meaningless task for all eternity. Does he meditate on the meaninglessness of life, how everything he does is pointless? How does he cope? How does he wake up every day to a life that is so absurd? This is not a journey where he conquers evil and succeeds or where he is being tested by God.

He accomplishes nothing. His whole life is a failure. So how does he make meaning out of such meaninglessness? By extension, Camus is saying that this is how our lives are. We strive to achieve goals, but these all come to nothing because we ultimately die. We fail. So what do we do—give up?

Camus suggests that an existentialist approach is the method to create meaning in such an absurd situation. Sisyphus has to make the absurd task meaningful. He acts, to the absolute best of his ability, as if life has meaning.

In other words, he fails brilliantly.

In terms of first-degree failures, all we can do within this worldview is accept the tragic failure and press on. We make meaning out of meaninglessness. If we fail, if we let the rock roll down the hill, we do not stamp our feet or cry or give up; we doggedly go back down and roll it up again. We know we will fail, but we also know that this is life, and we will come to accept failure as a norm. We own it. We make it part of our lives, day in, day out.

> His fate belongs to him. His rock is his thing. . . . The absurd man says yes and his effort will henceforth be unceasing. If there is a personal fate, there is no higher destiny. . . . The struggle itself toward the heights is enough to fill a man's heart. One must imagine Sisyphus happy.[10]

Camus argues that by taking hold of our actions and acknowledging that we live an absurd life, the failures of our lives will become meaningful: We own these failures. They make us who we are.

The message is: suck it up, because there's nothing you can do. From this point of view, failure is just the bitter pill you swallow every day.

The value in this for anyone could be simply that sometimes, letting go of something we cannot change is the best thing to do rather than hitting our heads against a brick wall or railing against what will only stress and break us if we try to change it.

The Second Law of Thermodynamics states that there is a natural tendency of any isolated system to degenerate into a more disordered state anyway. The world has a propensity, in other words, to break down, to reach entropy—or, in our terms, to fail. We can no more argue against it than we can fight gravity.

Think of "Murphy's Law": if anything can go wrong, it will go wrong. There is no grand purpose, and we are on our own to muddle our way through and do the best we can. Life is hard, but we must make meaning of it as best we can.

# NEW AGE PHILOSOPHIES AND POSITIVE THINKING

Many modern philosophies embrace a more positive view on failure, an optimistic worldview that argues that we can change any circumstances and are empowered through our will and reasoning to avoid or transform failure into success. The myriad of New Age philosophies embrace a spirituality and a general Way or Path. They invoke trust in the universe, that there is a plan, that all is connected. Many New Age philosophies argue that dwelling on anything negative, such as failure, is bad, because in so doing, we attract failure and need to think our way out of failure and negative thinking.

At nine years old, our son James was very enthusiastic about mowing the lawn. When he visited his grandparents and found they owned an electric mower—the type with an extension cord you had to plug into a power outlet and drag around the yard with you—he wanted to try it out. But his grandparents were very concerned and yelled instructions to him as he began to mow. "Don't ride over the power cable while you're mowing!" And because he turned to listen to what they were saying, he did exactly that. There was a loud bang, fizz, and smoke as the mower short-circuited, and he had done the very thing they feared would happen. The moral of that story: the more you fear failure, the more you dwell on it, the more likely it is to happen.

Sigmund Freud is rumoured to have told the following story about two young children who were going to have a visit from the new pastor of the church. Their mother warned them that he was very conscious of his rather large nose and under no circumstances were they to mention his nose, or stare at it, or giggle. The girls dutifully promised and all went well until one daughter offered him tea. "Would you like some sugar in your nose?" she said. "I mean tea."

Freud used this story to illustrate how repressed desires surface in what are now called "Freudian slips." But the story also illustrates how we will fall into a gravitational pull of our own failure.

We often experience this: We must sleep the night before an important day at the office, so we lie awake all night. We must remember a crucial thing for an important speech we are giving, so we go blank. How do we avoid this unconscious slide into failure because of our very fear of failure? Relax, accept, acknowledge our weaknesses, and don't try so hard to avoid them.

Conversely, according to these philosophies, a focus on success can lead to more positive results. Marty McFly's father reminds us of the American dream: "You can do anything if you set your mind to it."

Mindfulness, positive thinking, and conscious living offer New Age perspectives that suggest failure is a state of mind and we can harness the powers of the universe to overcome it, succeed, and be who we were meant to be.

Positive thinking takes a lot of people a long way. Norman Vincent Peale's self-help book *The Power of Positive Thinking*[11] influenced generations of people who used this power to conquer negative attitudes that cause failure. But then a shadow falls on millions of people who encounter unexpected misfortunes and outcomes despite their positive thinking: "This must be my fault. I am a weak and useless positive thinker. I clearly haven't done enough positive thinking. I have drawn all this bad stuff to me, so somehow I must deserve it." And that is neither a comforting nor helpful story.

In an article on "mindless optimism," Andy Martin argues that we are suffering "the Hawaiianisation of everywhere," a "mindless optimism" that needs to be deconstructed if we are to deal with failure.

> Understanding why we are so miserable should liberate us from being too miserable about it. We can feel good about feeling bad. In other words, we need a decent philosophy of failure to save everyone from thinking what failures they are.[12]

# ZEN AND THE ART OF FAILURE

Robert Pirsig's groundbreaking 1974 novel *Zen and the Art of Motorcycle Maintenance: An Inquiry into Values* provides a quirky modern philosophy and a valuable discussion of failure. In this unusual and very readable philosophical novel, Pirsig uses the framework of repairing and maintaining a motorcycle to philosophise about life in general. The novel attempts to answer the big question: *How do we deal with failure?* The answer? We need what Pirsig calls "gumption."

> If you're going to repair a motorcycle, an adequate supply of gumption is the first and most important tool. If you haven't got that, you might as well gather up all the other tools and put them away, because they won't do you any good. Gumption is the psychic

gasoline that keeps the whole thing going. If you haven't got it, there's no way the motorcycle can possibly be fixed. But if you have got it and know how to keep it, there's absolutely no way in this whole world that motorcycle can keep from getting fixed. It's bound to happen. Therefore, the thing that must be monitored at all times and preserved before anything else is . . . gumption. . . .

Throughout the process of fixing the machine, things always come up, low-quality things, from a dusted knuckle to an accidentally ruined "irreplaceable" assembly. These drain off gumption, destroy enthusiasm, and leave you so discouraged you want to forget the whole business. I call these things "gumption traps."[13]

Pirsig describes how we need to persevere in the face of adversity and use our "common sense, shrewdness, and a sense of initiative" to avoid a "negative feedback loop" that wants us to resign ourselves to failure and pessimism and defeat. Once we know this "trap," we can overcome it. The psychologist Martin Seligman called this gumption trap *learned helplessness*, where a person gives up trying.[14] Feelings of failure, as we know from earlier chapters, tend to create a psychic loop. We feel more and more like a failure and so will become more and more likely to "fail." But by harnessing "gumption," we can break out of this cycle.

So hopefully it's obvious by now that the stories we tell ourselves about our failures are determined by our belief system, our philosophy of life. Most people aren't aware that they are living according to a particular philosophy, but we all are. With this in mind, we can see failure as a mistake, a challenge, an inevitable part of the fabric of the universe. But failure is, above all, not a fixed, objective "thing." Failure is a *concept*, and we can rearrange how we perceive it. We are not locked into any world-view or philosophical outlook. By looking at more and more diverse worldviews and seeing them as frameworks rather than as The Truth, we can loosen their hold on us and free ourselves to think outside the prisons of genetic and social determinism.

"We will all end in failure, but that's not the most important thing," Costica Bradatan says. "What really matters is *how* we fail, and what we gain in the process."[15]

## BIG IDEAS AND HELPFUL THOUGHTS FROM THE DIFFERENT PHILOSOPHIES OF FAILURE

- ▶ **Buddhism:** Let go of your desires and the idealistic worldviews that blind you to enjoying what you do have.
- ▶ **Platonism:** Perfection in this world is unattainable. All your material failures and successes are shadows you make in your virtual cave.
- ▶ **Hellenistic philosophies:** There is an art to negotiating your lives around the obstacles and failures you encounter. You can make your lives happy in spite of failure.
- ▶ **Religious worldviews:** There is a higher purpose for all failures; accept this life's failings as part of a bigger plan.
- ▶ **Existentialism:** Make the most of what you have and are given in life. Create meaning out of the so-called failures of your circumstances.
- ▶ **Zen:** Avoid cyclic gumption traps that make you feel like you are a failure. Take practical steps to avoid the pitfalls of failure behaviour:
    1. Figure out what went wrong.
    2. Make a plan to prevent the mistake in the future.
    3. View each mistake as temporary and isolated.

## NOTES

1. Harry and June Webster. Interview with the authors, 2016. Names changed for privacy.

2. Conlon, Michael. "Writer Cormac McCarthy confides in Oprah Winfrey." *Reuters* Entertainment, June 5, 2007. Accessed March 6, 2017. http://www.reuters.com/article/2007/06/05/us-mccarthy-idUSN0526436120070605.

3. Konstan, David. "Epicurus." *Stanford Encyclopedia of Philosophy*, Fall 2016 edition. Edited by Edward N. Zalta. Accessed March 6, 2017. https://plato.stanford.edu/entries/epicurus.

4. Seneca. "On Peace of Mind." *The Stoics Reader: Selected Writings and Testimonia*. Translated by Brad Inwood and Lloyd P. Gerson. Cambridge, MA: Hackett Publishing Company, 2008.

5. AFP. "'Miracle baby' survives 11-story fall from apartment window in Minnesota," *The Telegraph*, May 15, 2014. Accessed March 7, 2017. http://www.telegraph.co.uk/news/worldnews/northamerica/usa/10832517/Miracle-baby-survives-11-story-fall-from-apartment-window-in-Minnesota.html.

6. Shum, David. "Boy, 12, survives fall from 6th floor apartment balcony in North York." *Global News*, January 12, 2017. Accessed March 7, 2017. http://globalnews.ca/news/3176549/child-injured-after-falling-from-apartment-balcony-in-north-toronto/.

7. Bradatan, Costica. "In Praise of Failure." *New York Times*, December 15, 2013. https://opinionator.blogs.nytimes.com/2013/12/15/in-praise-of-failure/?_r=0.

8. Horrigan, Paul Gerald. "Sartre's Atheistic Existentialism." *God's Existence and Other Philosophical Essays*. Bloomington, IN: iUniverse, 2007. http://www.academia.edu/9966165/Sartres_Atheistic_Existentialism.

9. Solomon, Robert. *From Rationalism to Existentialism: The Existentialists and Their Nineteenth-Century Backgrounds*. Lanham, MD: Rowman & Littlefield Publishers, 2001. 279.

10. Camus, Albert. *The Myth of Sisyphus*. Translated by Justin O'Brien. London: Hamish Hamilton Limited, 1955.

11. Peale, Norman Vincent. *The Power of Positive Thinking*. New York: Touchstone, 2003.

12. Martin, Andy. "Against happiness: Why we need a philosophy of failure." *Prospect* magazine, August 1, 2014. Accessed March 6, 2017. http://www.prospectmagazine.co.uk/arts-and-books/against-happiness-why-we-need-a-philosophy-of-failure.

13. Pirsig, Robert M. *Zen and the Art of Motorcycle Maintenance: An Inquiry into Values.* New York: Vintage, 2004. 286–287.

14. Seligman, Martin E. P. "Learned Helplessness." *Annual Review of Medicine* 23, no. 1 (1972): 407–12. Accessed March 6, 2017. http://www.annualreviews.org/doi/abs/10.1146/annurev.me.23.020172.002203.

15. Bradatan, "In Praise of Failure."

# CHAPTER TEN

# TRANSFORMATIVE THINKING:

## THE ERASURE OF FAILURE

R egardless of which philosophical worldviews we hold, and regardless of our views on life and failure, consider this: as long as we live and evolve as humans on this planet, we will be part of a process of trial and error in every aspect of our lives. After all, that's what's been happening on the planet for the past four billion years. It is likely to continue for some time.

As a species, we will sometimes reach the goals we set ourselves, and then we will evolve new ones and keep reaching. We will fall short of others, and sometimes we will discover entirely new things while we are searching for something else.

In the last two hundred years, we have slowly turned the word and the concept of *failure* into something terrifying that keeps our children, our doctors and surgeons, and so many of us so fearful that we will do anything in our lives to avoid being labelled "failures." It's clear from looking at the books and articles advocating the merits of failure in science and innovation that there is a movement to see the value in failure, and we think this is a start. But as long as we are bound by the word *failure* and the present-day connotations of the term, it seems unlikely that we will escape the shadow of failure when it falls on us, when we are labelled or when we label others as "being a failure." This has led to many of the contemporary stresses that negatively affect our lives: our children would sometimes rather die than fail; our doctors would rather hide the truth than look like failures; as employees, we would rather cover our errors than look like we've made mistakes.

"Fail" is never far from our everyday conversations. We hear it on television, at work, at school, and in our personal relationships. The result all too often leads to feelings of being unworthy and not as good as the next guy. But when we start erasing the language and concept of failure, the focus is redesigned. No one fails. Everyone sits at a point along a continuum. The colleges who have eliminated the idea of failure quite successfully are Reed College in Oregon, New College in Florida, and Evergreen College in Washington. These places give us hope. We could incorporate such an approach in all education and in other areas of our lives. At these colleges, which don't use failure as a threat of extinction, students excel and go on to become lawyers, doctors, journalists, social workers, etc. We have enough evidence that we no longer have any need for a carrot-and-stick industrial model, which sees students as potential economic units needing to be prodded along to fill gaps in the workforce. That's long over. It's time for us, regardless of our philosophies and narratives, to erase failure from the realms of education and human endeavour. If we talk about unexpected outcomes rather than failure, we more accurately and helpfully represent what is going on in society when young people learn, when explorers set out, when inventors invent. These humans are not failing. They should not ever be thinking of themselves in terms of failure. Our students and scientists and entrepreneurs are hard at work the world over, discovering the hundred ways that things don't work and the potential for unexpected advances from experimenting and playing. They are learning from trying things out. Some of them move through experiences quickly, while others develop more slowly, with interesting and unplanned revelations developing along the way. Our language and philosophies need to reflect that.

It seems that if we can change the way we perceive failure throughout our lives, we can erase the emotional and psychological pain associated with the stigma that comes when we say that something or someone is a failure.

If we believe in life as a series of steps on a ladder to the top, then most of us are failures, but if we take away the ladder, no one's a failure! We're just all at different points along a continuum. Life is a story, not a race.

It's time to replace fear with love and hope, and with aspirations for personal meaning and fulfilment that don't rely on measurable, material, or monetary gains.

Imagine if we stop destroying ourselves and our colleagues, our employees and employers, our partners and families with concepts that fill everyone with the fear of falling short. When we live with the concept of failure, we kill the natural curiosity that has allowed our species to evolve in such spectacular ways. For our future to truly be better and brighter and more hopeful, we have to stop suffocating the curiosity of the millions of children, of all the creative and innovative humans, who are trying to learn to adapt to a world whose future we cannot yet imagine.

Our first-degree failures are our most difficult, because they are catastrophic. Still, with this new approach to second- and third-degree failures, we can begin to see that the more open we are to understanding that unexpected outcomes are a *guaranteed experience* if we are alive on the planet, the more we can attempt to learn from these failures and continue to live meaningful lives, even with their effects. Whether we are religious or atheist or agnostic, we face the reality of things turning out differently than we anticipated. We are human, and our time on the planet is finite, but most of us would like to get the most out of that time, and this may be one way of doing it.

Our pursuit of success, our drive to set goals and achieve more and more of whatever it is we're pursuing, has led us to fear or bury our "failure," when the reality of an unexpected outcome is full of intrinsic value that cannot be seen when it's called a failure. This is why the literature on "fail better/faster/sooner" doesn't go far enough. That worldview is a good step. It attempts to reassign a positive value to the experiences we call failure . . . but invariably, our whole society continues to judge and mark itself on a success/failure basis in which failure almost always carries with it resultant shame and blame.

We need to take a radical position on our old understanding and use of the word *failure*, and this transition to a new point of view may be challenging for some people. It may shake previously held beliefs. But that's great, because if we can consider that our success/failure continuum is just a narrative that we've constructed, then we're free. We might not ever be able to look at education or the entire realm of human endeavour with the same eyes. And that might liberate us to do things and be things and make strides in education, business, medicine, and our own lives, which serve us well. It may change how we view our goals and how we think about personal success.

Once we step into a new way of looking at the unexpected outcomes in our lives, many things may change. For example, someone who previously held beliefs or made assumptions such as "It's terrible to fail, and my goal is to succeed at everything I do" might change their personal approach to "To live is to contend with unexpected outcomes, and I am wisely equipped to manage the challenges that come my way."

Changing an attitude could result in a transformed way of dealing with even the smallest unexpected outcome, such as the way you react when your kid spills his juice over the book you're reading. Instead of "You're so clumsy, Dylan!" (in other words, "You've failed, kid!"), you might say, "Oops! Hey, Dylan, let's go get the cloth and clean this up" ("We're just going to deal with this unexpected turn of events in the best way we can").

Here are the thoughts of a few people who have found ways of contending with life's curveballs, from first- to third-degree failures.

Michelle Gerard[1] told us that a recent event changed how she responded to ordinary unwanted experiences. Her kids had just moved out, and she decided she was going to buy herself a lovely little car, just for her, after her daughters had trashed hers over the years by learning to drive, taking themselves to school, to sports, to music performances. Now she was into a new phase, and her new car represented her newfound freedom. She was possessive of the car, didn't even want her husband to drive it, and loved it more than she had loved any other material thing for a while.

And then she came out one day and saw that someone had driven into it while she was parked, perhaps at the shopping centre. They had bashed it, scratched it, damaged it horribly. She was outraged. She said, "I couldn't believe they did that! They didn't have the courtesy to even leave their number!" She said she spent a good while ranting at the awfulness of these people, at the injustice of it all, and then she stopped.

> I realised the car was just a thing. That I was getting emotional about a thing and about an event that I couldn't do anything about. Then something happened: materialism lost its hold on me. I just let it all go. It's not worth the stress. It's just a car. I'm fine with what happened now. I like my car, but I'm happy for anyone to drive it and I am not going to invest myself in material things.

Jules Berstein[2] lives in California. When he first enrolled at university to do a degree in architecture, he was stressed, having already failed to complete an engineering degree and having dropped out a couple of years prior.

> I was getting very hyped up. I started school, and within about three months, I had my first manic episode—I freaked out. I was manic. I had visions of grandeur. It was an out-of-body experience with extreme paranoia. You think that everything is coming for you; you even think you're moving people around with your eyes— that you have this power. I talked a lot. Mostly garbage.
>
> I had all the symptoms of being bipolar but was undiagnosed. It was so extreme I left school, and that was a big black mark in my life. It's haunted me ever since.

Jules's life did not get any easier. He met a beautiful girl and was finally diagnosed with bipolar disorder and put on medication, but he lost his job and tried to commit suicide by cutting his own throat. When he recovered, he and his girlfriend eventually got married and had two children, but when the children were ten and thirteen, his wife died of breast cancer.

Incredibly, once alone with the kids, he never had another episode. It was survival, he said. But he'd learned a few things:

"Firstly, even though I had so much stress, and stress is usually a trigger, somehow I managed to avoid an episode—I was totally focused on the kids, and it became a question of survival. I don't think I had time to even grieve—I was just determined to survive." He says he believes his kids were guardian angels. He had to be there for them; he could not lose control.

Secondly, he learned something else. He knew that the world looked totally different when he was manic and when he was depressed, so when he recently went into a deep depression, he had the ability to be metacognitive and say that he knew this lesson well: "Life has taught me that things do eventually turn around. If it's mood related, that state colours your world. I was able to weather this [recent depression] storm. Because even in the deepest depression, there's been a glimmer of hope, however slight." He said understanding how different states of mind can colour his world enables him to "not go there again."

Perhaps the Buddhists were right about this: our distress for most of life's so-called failures lies in the gap between What We Want Things to Be and What Things Actually Are.

What if we are flexible with our thoughts and recognise that we need to make the most of every situation because we understand that there is much in the world over which we have little control?

# ERASING FAILURE

Let's imagine eliminating the word and concept of "failure" from our discourse. The very real experiences of disappointment, sadness, and struggles we have with our unexpected outcomes will still be there, but we can reshape our narratives and therefore our responses.

Peter Pretorius was born in South Africa. He started walking at nine months and was a healthy, happy boy in 1959. Then, when he was two years old, the week that his sisters were immunized against polio, he was ill with the flu and didn't get the vaccine. Two months later, his mother awoke one morning and found him lying paralysed in his crib. He had contracted polio. Terrified, she rushed him to hospital, where he was placed in an iron lung. His right side was affected badly, but after many weeks, the left side recovered somewhat. Polio attacks muscles but also the nerves connecting those muscles to the brain. He lost most of the use of his right leg, and his right side was very weak. As a toddler, he had to learn to walk with prosthetics, which were not very sophisticated during the 1960s. Still, he had a fairly strong left leg, and he bravely soldiered on. That would have been enough suffering for anyone, especially a small boy. But then another disaster struck.

> When I was eight, I went in for an operation on my left leg (my strong leg) to remove tissue to transplant to the weak leg. At the time, I had a boil on my knee, which I showed to the doctor before the operation. He was unconcerned. During the operation, however, they lacerated the boil, the infection went into the operation wound, and two days later, my toes turned blue. I was rushed to the hospital with gangrene. After three months in the hospital, my left leg—my strong leg—had to be amputated.[3]

The thing about life is, once something irreversible has happened, what do we do? We can sue people, rage against the reality, live in regret and remorse and anger and blame, but the fact is, some things cannot be altered. This turn of events was devastating for Peter. This should never have happened. It was unnecessary, cruel. The consequences were life-changing. Now the young boy was even further disabled than before.

The world can be appallingly unfair.

Bad things do happen to good people.

And whether we believe this is the result of God's plan for us and that there will be rewards later in the afterlife, or whether you believe this is a random act of destiny without any meaning except the one we make of it, one thing's for sure: none of us are immune to suffering.

And so, eventually, our only option is how we face catastrophes, how we live with the things we wish never happened.

Some people grow bitter. Some sink into depression.

Peter could have become bitter, depressed, suicidal even. He didn't. He looked to the skies. He watched planes flying overhead and he thought, *Well, what about flying?* If he couldn't walk, why couldn't he fly? He spent his childhood dreaming of owning his own plane, of flying high above life's mundane humps and bumps, and he wasn't going to be put off by anyone.

He had a long, hard journey in those days. At first there seemed to be no way he would pass his medical exam. All kinds of excuses were thrown at him as to why he could not get his pilot's license. But he would not give up. He had to prove that he could fly a normal plane with his prosthetics and show that he could exit the plane as quickly as an able-bodied person in an emergency. He did it.

> Finally, after five years, I was a pilot who could fly a normal plane. I had also wanted to champion disabled people to enjoy the same activities as those who are able bodied. Two years later, I received an instructor's rating. Two years after that, I became a Certified Flying Instructor with my own flying school. I was one of the first paraplegic flying instructors in the world. To date, I've trained over 400 pilots.

Peter's message is one of hope, of not giving in to despair. When the ground could not support him, he looked somewhere else. The skies welcomed him, and he found his place.

Today, Peter lives in Australia, flies his plane on the weekends, and inspires people at Rotary clubs and schools with his motivational talks on living with and dealing with the curveballs that life can throw anyone at any time.

He isn't world-famous yet, but in our opinion, he should be.

What Peter has to say about life and struggle is worth listening to. His has been a life marked by extreme adversity. His smile and positive outlook, his great sense of humour and sunny disposition, would inspire anyone to get out of bed every day and face the world with courage.

So the truest thing we can say is: life will throw unexpected outcomes at us. We will face loss. We will face injustice somewhere along the line.

Sometimes we get a come-around from out of the blue. A first-degree failure. A catastrophe we didn't see coming. An irreparable loss.

If we believe that our lives have intrinsic value, regardless of how challenging or hard they are—if we believe that we are valuable and worth it—our only choice is to find the gumption, the guts, the courage, the ways to live with and beyond unanticipated events. Whether they are failed exams, failed marriages, or cars or planes which fail to arrive at their destinations, we have a choice: rage against life or spend time developing deep resilience—ways to move on, move forward and live, because our lives are precious.

There is no room in Peter's life for a thing called "failure."

When we erase failure, we are not obliterating our capacity to miss the mark. We can't. We will fall and stumble every day along the way. This is part of life. On the contrary, we're erasing a narrow set of margins that box us in as "failures" with far-reaching negative consequences.

We are brilliant human beings. We have the capacity to evolve. We transform. But often, DNA doesn't replicate properly, and we have to live with that. Sometimes things unravel. Sometimes—many times—our lives don't go according to plan. We are all getting older, yet our bodies are primed to heal and balance themselves along the way. Everything decays, yet repair is part of all our evolution. When we get rid of the language of failure, we eliminate judgment. We dissolve the pain that comes to so many of us because we place certain people at the top of a ladder and others at the bottom. We look at the unexpected and unanticipated and accept that this is an intrinsic part of life. We stop judging ourselves in comparison to others and begin to look at the true value of our own lives. This is even possible with tragic first-degree failures. June's story is a prime example:

Many years ago, June Wilson[4] experienced one of the worst tragedies imaginable, the loss of her six-year-old in a bicycle accident. Her youngest son was cycling up and down their quiet street in California when a car came around the corner too fast, oversteered, and knocked the boy off his bike. He died in the hospital hours later. Despite the fact that this accident happened over forty years ago, June says she still feels the pain acutely. "It never goes away," she said.

> The only thing I can tell you is that I realised this one thing: who was I to ever think that I would be protected from suffering? None of us have any guarantees. This is life. And this loss is a part of mine. And a part of many people's lives. It is happening today, and will happen tomorrow, and millions of us will struggle to live with our grief and find ways to get up in the morning and love and care for those left behind.

She has found meaning over the years working for a philanthropic organisation and for charities, helping those in need, winning awards for her work, and helping families facing financial and personal crises. She took her grief and her helplessness and used them to motivate her to help where she had the power to do so and to be empathetic to those experiencing loss of all kinds. She made things easier and lighter for so many people, and this gave meaning to her existence. She honoured her son's memory by helping other children wherever she could.

The gift June gives to us, just as Pete does, is courage and an understanding of the way life is.

These things will happen. None of us are any more protected than June from suffering or from the impacts of tragedy on our lives. Once we know this, we can begin to appreciate everything. We can treasure the time we have with our families, appreciate the challenges that come our way, enjoy our journey, and develop the strengths and skills we need when life throws us really difficult things.

Without the concept of "failure" hanging over our lives, we give ourselves the opportunity to become more truly ourselves, because unexpected outcomes demand of us that we become flexible, empathetic, creative, and innovative—not just in a material sense but emotionally, psychologically, spiritually. We have to become our best human selves, draw on all our resources. We were made for this world. We are part of a grand, evolving universe.

"Failure" is a small-minded concept that we throw over aspects of our lives and then believe in as though it is absolute reality. It is a mere shadow on the wall of Plato's Cave.

If we erase failure, blame has to go with it. Blame is the god-child of failure. We blame others in order to make ourselves feel better, to put ourselves on the next level up in the pecking order. We are not as bad, as stupid as they are. When looking for a cause for an error, a failure, an accident, we feel the need to apportion blame to someone. This relieves us of our responsibility. But blame, even if the other party is indeed responsible for the error, does not make anything better. It does not help people "pull up their socks" nor does it undo damage. When we believe in failure, blame is never very far around the corner.

As a society, we are unconsciously failure- and blame-driven. Something or someone fails. There must be someone to blame. There are moves to transform this in certain areas, such as restorative justice in the criminal justice system and in education, but on the whole, we behave as though this is the way things are. Our need for transformative thinking around blame will help us in transforming our thinking about failure.

In an article in *Psychology Today*, Elliot Cohen says blame is based on a "series of four irrational beliefs," which are:

1. It's someone else's fault.
2. That person isn't worth respecting.
3. They should be treated badly.
4. I can't accept any degree of responsibility for this, otherwise I'm as worthless as the person I'm blaming.[5]

Here are some examples of the failure/blame relationship where there is really no logical connection between what is seen as cause and effect and which we need to overcome as we erase previously held beliefs about failure:

- I failed to get the promotion, therefore my boss is a woman-hater.
- I failed to get that house deal, therefore the real estate agent is an idiot.
- He had to go off and have an affair because his wife wasn't interesting to him anymore.
- He took out a loan and gambled because he was feeling trapped in his relationship.

When we feel that we've "failed," we often just want someone else to shoulder the responsibility. But we have to step out of the shame/blame cave of shadows because it doesn't help anyone, least of all ourselves.

A restorative approach, for example, sees the world differently: the wrong thing is defined as that which causes harm. Acts that cause harm create responsibility and liability. Therefore, if someone really did do something wrong, they are responsible for making things right.

Peter could have blamed the surgeon whose error of judgment led to him losing his good leg. He could have anguished over that all his life. He didn't.

A tragic event occurred on August 25th, 1993, in South Africa just as Apartheid was ending. A young American Fulbright scholar, Amy Biehl, passionate about human rights, was taking her friends back to their township home in Gugulethu (near Cape Town) the night before she was due to fly back to California. As she drove them home that evening, the car passed a gathering of youths who had just emerged from a volatile political meeting. They saw her white skin and blonde hair and attacked the car with rocks. Seeing her way was blocked, she exited the car in an attempt to escape. A group of young men chased her, caught her, and stabbed her to death.

It seems unimaginable that forgiveness under such circumstances could be possible. But this is exactly the response from Amy's parents.

Linda and Peter Biehl flew to South Africa to find out what exactly had happened to their daughter. Linda writes in The Forgiveness Project:

> When we heard the terrible news about Amy the whole family was devastated, but at the same time we wanted to understand the circumstances surrounding her death. Soon afterwards we left for Cape Town. We took our strength in handling the situation directly from Amy. She was intensely involved in South African politics and even though the violence leading up to free elections had caused her death, we didn't want to say anything negative about South Africa's journey to democracy. Therefore, in 1998, when the four men convicted of her murder applied for amnesty, we did not oppose it. At the amnesty hearing we shook hands with the families of the perpetrators.[6]

Linda and Peter set up a foundation in Amy's honour to continue their daughter's work, fighting for the rights of the destitute, the disempowered youth. Two of the men who began to work for the foundation were her killers. Linda says of them: "I've grown fond of these young men. They're like my own kids. It may sound strange, but I tend to think there's a little bit of Amy's spirit in them. Some people think we are supporting criminals, but the Foundation that we started in her name is all about preventing crime among youth. I have come to believe passionately in restorative justice. It's what Desmond Tutu calls 'ubuntu': to choose to forgive rather than demand retribution, a belief that 'my humanity is inextricably caught up in yours.'"[7]

Easy Nofemela, one of Amy's killers, said:

Not until I met Linda and Peter Biehl did I understand that white people are human beings too. I was a member of Azanian People's Liberation Army, the armed wing of the Pan Africanist Congress. Our slogan was "one settler, one bullet." The first time I saw them on TV I hated them. I thought this was the strategy of the white [parents], to come to South Africa to call for capital punishment. But they didn't even mention wanting to hang us. I was very confused. They seemed to understand that the youth of the townships had carried this crisis—this fight for liberation—on their shoulders.

At first I didn't want to go to the Truth and Reconciliation Commission to give my testimony. I thought it was a sell-out, but then I read in the press that Linda and Peter had said that it was not up to them to forgive: it was up to the people in South Africa to learn to forgive each other. I decided to go and tell our story and show remorse. Amnesty wasn't my motivation. I just wanted to ask for forgiveness. I wanted to say in front of Linda and Peter, face to face, "I am sorry; can you forgive me?" I wanted to be free in my mind and body. It must have been so painful for them to lose their daughter, but by coming to South Africa—not to speak of recrimination, but to speak of the pain of our struggle—they gave me back my freedom. I am not a killer, I have never thought of myself as such, but I will never belong to a political organisation again, because such organisations dictate your thoughts and actions.[8]

This response to an irreversible first-degree failure provides evidence of a very different way of responding to a tragic event, rather than revenge and the desire for some kind of payback.

This does not bring people back, though it may make people feel their loved ones have not died for nothing.

In the case of this well-known personal catastrophe involving Amy Biehl, her family exemplified a deeply moving and inspiring approach to irreparable loss. They showed forgiveness, resulting in social renewal and redemption instead of incarceration and punishment for the perpetrators of a horrific crime.

In the end, it's about our own choices. We might ask this essential question: what outcome do we want?

If our impulse is to hit back and seek revenge, the questions to ask are these:

What does such action result in for our lives? Does it resolve the issue? Does it ease the pain of losing a loved person? Does it make life easier afterwards? Oftentimes it does not, but it begins a spiral of hatred and bitterness and a sense of how unfair life has been.

But if we seek to reframe such "failures," we may find that they lead to positive outcomes that help us heal the wounds more quickly than an impulse for retribution.

Linda and Peter Biehl could have cried out for "justice" or "revenge." But their daughter was already dead. No kind of justice would bring her back. Her parents knew their daughter, and they knew what she believed in: she wanted violence against humanity to end. Creating the Amy Foundation helped bring meaning not only to their lives but to the lives of Amy's killers and countless disadvantaged youth that the Foundation supports.

Every day, things go wrong. Planes crash. Buildings burn. People are lost. We can learn from errors, but only as long as we are prepared to acknowledge them, and the learning doesn't bring back what was lost. We still have to live with loss. There has to be accountability and responsibility and, where possible, restoring or repairing harm as far as possible. Blame just chases us all into hiding, and we disguise our errors and so-called failures and lie to preserve our dignity.

So let's imagine we erase failure as we've known it from every adventure or human endeavour. If you set out to design a new kind of airplane and it doesn't work, but you learn some subtle and fundamental things about lift and drag, that's awesome. You'll have knowledge and experience if you tackle this again or even if you decide to design cars or boats instead of planes. The hard-won knowledge is transferable physics. Or maybe you've been challenged to make a bicycle with square wheels work; you make the bike, and it doesn't work, but it becomes a statement, a sculpture in a modern art museum or a book cover commenting on the intrinsic beauty of so-called failed human endeavour. Or you go climb Mt. Everest and you make it to base camp, but you're getting sick and you have to cancel the climb before you've even begun. So what? You've tried. You've struggled. In all these scenarios, you journeyed. You had courage. You are a hero no matter what.

Value the qualities that you get from the challenges, the disappointments. This is your miraculous existence—and if life is made up of these outcomes previously called "failures," then fail—or, rather, *live* brilliantly in the time you have, knowing you are a part of the wider, unpredictable, evolving universe.

## BIG IDEAS

▶ What if we erase the idea of failure in the entire realm of human endeavour? We're not failing. We're discovering a hundred ways that things don't work.

▶ Our pursuit of success has led us to fear or bury our "failure" so that we cannot get any value out of the experience of an unexpected outcome.

▶ Once we get rid of old ideas of "failure," we give ourselves the opportunity to become more truly ourselves: unexpected outcomes demand of us that we become flexible, creative, innovative.

- Transforming our thoughts on failure is a threshold experience. Once we look at it in a new way, there's no going back.
- If we get rid of old ideas of failure, shame and blame can disappear with it.

## HELPFUL THOUGHTS ON TRANSFORMATIVE THINKING ABOUT FAILURE

- Remember: we were made for this world. We are part of a grand, evolving, and surprising universe.
- "Failure" is a small-minded concept that we throw over a section of our lives and then believe in it as though it is absolute reality. It's not.
- Stop comparing your life as it is to your life as you think it should be. Replace fear with love. Be the most authentic person you can be even when things don't turn out the way you'd hoped.
- Stop blaming others. Own your life. When unexpected things happen, look instead for how to repair things, or how to ensure others repair things, rather than shaming or blaming someone.
- Take hold of your life with both hands. When life doesn't go according to plan, remember you are still the same brilliant person. Your "failures" are now transformed in your mind to your "unexpected outcomes," and those can be managed.

## NOTES

1. Michelle Gerard. Interview with the authors, December 2016. Name changed for privacy.
2. Jules Berstein. Interview with the authors, January 2017. Name changed for privacy.

3. Pretorius, Peter, and Shelley Davidow. "Wings to Fly: A paraplegic's tenacious journey to the skies." *Plane & Pilot*, June 25, 2013. Accessed March 8, 2017. http://www.planeandpilotmag.com/article/wings-to-fly/#.WHhPXH1p9Va.

4. June Wilson. Interview with the authors, January 2017. Name changed for privacy.

5. Cohen, Elliot D. "Stop Playing the Blame Game: How Your Blame Claims May Be Impeding Happiness." *Psychology Today*, July 29, 2012. https://www.psychologytoday.com/blog/what-would-aristotle-do/201207/stop-playing-the-blame-game.

6. "Linda Biehl & Easy Nofemela (South Africa)." The Forgiveness Project, March 29, 2010. Accessed March 17, 2017. http://theforgivenessproject.com/stories/linda-biehl-easy-nofemela-south-africa/.

7. Ibid.

8. Ibid.

# LIVING WITH UNEXPECTED OUTCOMES

**F**ailure, as we've now discovered, is not a single concept to be feared and avoided at all costs. First-degree failures are disastrous; we cannot avoid them and have to cope with them when they happen and live with their effects. Second-degree failures are challenges that we can meet if we stop thinking about them as failures. Third-degree failures are arbitrary, self-imposed, and set up by our own expectations—and we can remove our sense of self-worth from their outcomes. In all three categories of so-called failure, our philosophies, our narratives, and our approaches can profoundly change the way they affect us. Below you will find a toolbox with exercises that ask you to write and think about your life and its unexpected outcomes. We hope these tools empower you to navigate the territory of your brilliant and unique lives.

# EXERCISES FOR TURNING FAILURE INTO UNEXPECTED OUTCOMES

## EXERCISE ONE: LIFE

Write down three recent events that you think of as failures.
Here are three examples:

1. Lost the dream house through not acting quickly or efficiently.
2. Found myself in a dead-end job where the boss is awful.
3. Spent time on a higher degree that has not made any difference in terms of employability.

If you could find value in these experiences (lessons, insights, etc.), write them down.
Examples:

1. **Dream house:** Learned about gut instinct and how to pay attention to it.
2. **Dead-end job:** Realised that I am valuable and too big for the petty rules, etc., imposed on me every day. Beginning to think of looking for something else.
3. **Higher degree:** Read so many articles that opened new avenues of thought that make life more interesting.

## EXERCISE TWO: WORK

Think of a work situation you're in where you fear failure.

1. Imagine and write down the worst possible outcome. (For example: Get fired/replaced for underperformance.)
2. Imagine and write down the best possible outcome. (For example: Get promoted for record sales.)

3. Imagine and write down disasters you're not expecting. (For example: Get hit by a semi trailer while crossing the road.)

4. Imagine and write down something spectacular you're not expecting. (For example: Get randomly head-hunted by a casting agent and offered a movie deal.)

Once you have these narratives, you can write the rest of each story and follow these four threads.

Rather than expecting any of these outcomes, know that they, and many others you haven't imagined, are all possible. Aim for what you want, but understand fully how unexpected scenarios unfold. You are most empowered when you have developed muscle tone, when you have been busy writing narratives, acknowledging the unexpected, and finding ways to manage them every day.

## EXERCISE THREE: RELATIONSHIPS

Think of a relationship situation you're in where you fear failure.

Remember: these are not failures—just outcomes. If you don't work it out, you break up. If you work it out, new things are possible between you. There is always the possibility of something happening that you never expected.

1. Write down the worst possible outcome. (For example: Can't work it out and break up.)

2. Write down the best possible outcome. (For example: Find a new way of being together.)

3. Write down a terrible unexpected outcome. (For example: Partner or self dies suddenly or gets sick.)

4. Write down a dreamy unexpected outcome. (For example: Newfound love is as amazing as a first love ever was, only deeper).

Once you have these narratives, you can write the rest of each story and follow these four threads. So what happens with the worst possible outcome? What plans do you make to deal with this scenario? What happens with the best possible outcome? What do you do?

## EXERCISE FOUR: HEALTH

Remember, in the end, all our health fails. Survival is a myth. We all fail to survive one day. But what we can do is postpone that day for as long as possible and thrive in the meantime.

Think of a health situation where you fear a bad outcome.

1. Write down the worst possible outcome. (For example: Josh takes a PSA test and finds it is abnormally high.)
2. Write down the best possible outcome. (For example: He finds after a test that there is no cancer present, just an enlarged prostate, which his normal for his age.)
3. Write down a terrible unexpected outcome. (For example: He has prostate cancer, and it has spread into his bones.)
4. Write down a dreamy unexpected outcome. (For example: The high PSA was an anomaly, and in subsequent tests, it is normal.)

Once you have these narratives, follow each thread. What happens with the worst possible outcome? What plans do you make to deal with this scenario? What happens with the best possible outcome? What do you do?

## EXERCISE FIVE: THE "WHAT IF" GAME

This exercise is a practice run for creating a coping plan of action if unwanted outcomes affect your life. Write down three worst-case scenarios and a plan of action for what you would do if those happened. What if you lost your job/spouse/house? This goes to scary places, but these are the monsters that keep adults up in the middle of the night anyway, so it's worth writing these scary imaginings down; instead of thinking "This will never happen to me," imagine it could and what you would do if it did.

To those who have goals and resolutions that you are working towards with all their hearts, write down three of them. Then for each goal, imagine that something gets in the way and makes that particular goal unachievable. Make a positive plan of action for each one of those if things don't go according to plan.

By doing this, by confronting our hopes and fears head on, we can develop one of the qualities we need most in this world: courage. The courage to live life as fully as possible, knowing that there are things that happen that are beyond our control.

# HOW TO FAIL BRILLIANTLY: TO LIVE IS TO FAIL

- ▶ Don't buy the myth that we have to "succeed."
- ▶ Go for a long walk in nature and breathe in the present moment. You are miraculously alive—and yourself. Breathe joy into your veins simply for being. It is a gift.
- ▶ Play with your kids. Enjoy time that is not being used to get somewhere, to go to a class or a lesson or a competitive game. Draw, paint, cook, tell jokes—even lame ones.
- ▶ Spend time with friends.
- ▶ Once a week, write your children/spouse a note: tell them what you value about them and what you are thankful for about them in your life.
- ▶ Volunteer. Help those who are suffering anywhere you find them. Give of your time, but mostly, give of your heart. It's the most human thing you can do.
- ▶ If you are in a soulless job environment that is desperately competitive, disentangle your self-value from your material successes or failures. Look at jobs

elsewhere that more closely match who you are. Even if change can't happen now, see yourself as in process, moving into something new that is being created. You are evolving.

▶ Do all of the above things and release yourself from the stress of your own and others' expectations about who you should be. The moment is not fixed. It's just a snapshot. If you have children in competitive school environments, show them you value who they are, not what they achieve in terms of grades or awards.

▶ For second- and third-degree failures, remember that we can change the way we see failure. And when first-degree failures occur, understand that the nature of our universe and our own lives is unavoidably full of unpredictable events; our best ally against these events is courage and the knowledge that we share this reality with everyone else on the planet.

## ACKNOWLEDGEMENTS

We'd like to extend our gratitude to the people in both Australia and the USA who generously shared their personal experiences and stories of "unexpected outcomes" with us. To the hard-working team at Familius—Katharine Hale and Brooke Jorden, David Miles, Erika Riggs, and Christopher Robbins—thank you for your support and for making the world a better place, one book at a time.

# ABOUT THE AUTHORS

SHELLEY DAVIDOW, DCA, MSEd, is an internationally acclaimed author of forty-three books. Her recent nonfiction titles include *Whisperings in the Blood* (University of Queensland Press, Australia, 2016), *Playing with Words* (Palgrave Macmillan, UK, 2016) coauthored with Paul Williams, and *Raising Stress-Proof Kids* (Familius, USA, 2015). She lectures in the departments of Education and Creative Writing at the University of the Sunshine Coast in Australia.

For more information, visit www.shelleydavidow.com.

PAUL WILLIAMS, PhD, is an award-winning author of several books including the memoir *Soldier Blue* (New Africa Books, South Africa, 2008). He lives in Australia and coordinates the Creative Writing Program at the University of the Sunshine Coast. His latest book is *Playing with Words* (Palgrave Macmillan, UK, 2016) coauthored with Shelley Davidow. Explore his website to discover more: www.paul-a-williams.com

# ABOUT FAMILIUS

VISIT OUR WEBSITE: WWW.FAMILIUS.COM

## JOIN OUR FAMILY

There are lots of ways to connect with us! Subscribe to our news-letters at www.familius.com to receive uplifting daily inspiration, essays from our Pater Familius, a free ebook every month, and the first word on special discounts and Familius news.

## GET BULK DISCOUNTS

If you feel a few friends and family might benefit from what you've read, let us know and we'll be happy to provide you with quantity discounts. Simply email us at orders@familius.com.

## CONNECT

- ► Facebook: www.facebook.com/paterfamilius
- ► Twitter: @familiustalk, @paterfamilius1
- ► Pinterest: www.pinterest.com/familius
- ► Instagram: @familiustalk

THE MOST IMPORTANT WORK YOU
EVER DO WILL BE WITHIN THE WALLS
OF YOUR OWN HOME.

CPSIA information can be obtained
at www.ICGtesting.com
Printed in the USA
FSOW02n1012300617
35832FS